The Challenge of Peace:
God's Promise and Our Response

**A Pastoral Letter on
War and Peace**

May 3, 1983
National Conference of Catholic Bishops

Following the bishops' November, 1980 general meeting, a committee of bishops was appointed to draft a pastoral letter on war and peace. The first draft of this letter was submitted to the bishops in June, 1982, with subsequent drafts presented in November, 1982 and May, 1983. Approval of the text by the body of bishops was given during the plenary assembly in Chicago on May 3, 1983. Accordingly, publication of this pastoral letter is authorized by the undersigned.

June 23, 1983

Monsignor Daniel F. Hoye
General Secretary, NCCB/USCC

First Printing   July 8, 1983
Second Printing   August 12, 1983
Third Printing September 6, 1983
Fourth Printing   October 17, 1983
Fifth Printing   December 6, 1983

CONTENTS

Summary

The Second Vatican Council opened its evaluation of modern warfare with the statement: "The whole human race faces a moment of supreme crisis in its advance toward maturity." We agree with the council's assessment; the crisis of the moment is embodied in the threat which nuclear weapons pose for the world and much that we hold dear in the world. We have seen and felt the effects of the crisis of the nuclear age in the lives of people we serve. Nuclear weaponry has drastically changed the nature of warfare, and the arms race poses a threat to human life and human civilization which is without precedent.

We write this letter from the perspective of Catholic faith. Faith does not insulate us from the daily challenges of life but intensifies our desire to address them precisely in light of the gospel which has come to us in the person of the risen Christ. Through the resources of faith and reason we desire in this letter to provide hope for people in our day and direction toward a world freed of the nuclear threat.

As Catholic bishops we write this letter as an exercise of our teaching ministry. The Catholic tradition on war and peace is a long and complex one; it stretches from the Sermon on the Mount to the statements of Pope John Paul II. We wish to explore and explain the resources of the moral-religious teaching and to apply it to specific questions of our day. In doing this we realize, and we want readers of this letter to recognize, that not all statements in this letter have the same moral authority. At times we state universally binding moral principles found in the teaching of the Church; at other times the pastoral letter makes specific applications, observations and recommendations which allow for diversity of opinion on the part of those who assess the factual data of a situations differently. However, we expect Catholics to give our moral judgments serious consideration when they are forming their own views on specific problems. The experience of preparing this letter has manifested to us the range of strongly held opinion in the Catholic community on questions of fact and judgment concerning issues of war and peace. We urge mutual respect among individuals and groups in the Church as this letter is analyzed and discussed. Obviously, as bishops, we believe that such differences should be expressed within the framework of Catholic moral teaching. We need in the Church not only conviction and commitment but also civility and charity.

While this letter is addressed principally to the Catholic community, we want it to make a contribution to the wider public debate in our country on the dangers and dilemmas of the nuclear age. Our contribution will not be primarily technical or political, but we are convinced that there is no satisfactory answer to the human problems of the nuclear age which fails to consider the moral and religious dimensions of the questions we face.

Although we speak in our own name, as Catholic bishops of the Church in the United States, we have been conscious in the preparation of this letter of the consequences our teaching will have not only for the United States but for other nations as well. One important expression of this awareness has been the consultation we have had, by correspondence and in an important meeting held at the Vatican (January 18–19, 1983), with representatives of European bishops' conferences. This consultation with bishops of other countries, and, of course, with the Holy See, has been very helpful to us.

Catholic teaching has always understood peace in positive terms. In the words of Pope John Paul II: "Peace is not just the absence of war. . . . Like a cathedral, peace must be constructed patiently and with unshakable faith." (Coventry, England, 1982) Peace is the fruit of order. Order in human society must be shaped on the basis of respect for the transcendence of God and the unique dignity of each person, understood in terms of freedom, justice, truth and love. To avoid war in our day we must be intent on building peace in an increasingly interdependent world. In Part III of this letter we set forth a positive vision of peace and the demands such a vision makes on diplomacy, national policy, and personal choices.

While pursuing peace incessantly, it is also necessary to limit the use of force in a world comprised of nation states, faced with common problems but devoid of an adequate international political authority. Keeping the peace in the nuclear age is a moral and political imperative. In Parts I and II of this letter we set forth both the principles of Catholic teaching on war and a series of judgments, based on these principles, about concrete policies. In making these judgments we speak as moral teachers, not as technical experts.

I. Some Principles, Norms and Premises of Catholic Teaching

A. On War

1. Catholic teaching begins in every case with a presumption against war and for peaceful settlement of disputes. In exceptional cases, determined by the moral principles of the just-war tradition, some uses of force are permitted.
2. Every nation has a right and duty to defend itself against unjust aggression.
3. Offensive war of any kind is not morally justifiable.
4. It is never permitted to direct nuclear or conventional weapons to "the indiscriminate destruction of whole cities or vast areas with their populations. . . ." (*Pastoral Constitution*, #80.) The intentional killing of innocent civilians or non-combatants is always wrong.
5. Even defensive response to unjust attack can cause destruction which violates the principle of proportionality, going far beyond the limits of legitimate defense. This judgment is particularly important when assessing planned use of nuclear weapons. No defensive strategy, nuclear or conventional, which exceeds the limits of proportionality is morally permissible.

B. On Deterrence

1. "In current conditions 'deterrence' based on balance, certainly not as an end in itself but as a step on the way toward a progressive disarmament, may still be judged morally acceptable. Nonetheless, in order to ensure peace, it is indispensable not to be satisfied with this minimum which is always susceptible to the real danger of explosion." (Pope John Paul II, "Message to U.N. Special Session on Disarmament," #8, June 1982.)
2. No *use* of nuclear weapons which would violate the principles of discrimination or proportionality may be *intended* in a strategy of deterrence. The moral demands of Catholic teaching re-

quire resolute willingness not to intend or to do moral evil even to save our own lives or the lives of those we love.

3. Deterrence is not an adequate strategy as a long-term basis for peace; it is a transitional strategy justifiable only in conjunction with resolute determination to pursue arms control and disarmament. We are convinced that "the fundamental principle on which our present peace depends must be replaced by another, which declares that the true and solid peace of nations consists not in equality of arms but in mutual trust alone." (Pope John XXIII, *Peace on Earth*, #113.)

C. The Arms Race and Disarmament

1. The arms race is one of the greatest curses on the human race; it is to be condemned as a danger, an act of aggression against the poor, and a folly which does not provide the security it promises. (Cf: *Pastoral Constitution*, #81, *Statement of the Holy See to the United Nations*, 1976.)

2. Negotiations must be pursued in every reasonable form possible; they should be governed by the "demand that the arms race should cease; that the stockpiles which exist in various countries should be reduced equally and simultaneously by the parties concerned; that nuclear weapons should be banned; and that a general agreement should eventually be reached about progressive disarmament and an effective method of control." (Pope John XXIII, *Peace On Earth*, #112.)

D. On Personal Conscience

1. *Military Service:* "All those who enter the military service in loyalty to their country should look upon themselves as the custodians of the security and freedom of their fellow countrymen; and when they carry out their duty properly, they are contributing to the maintenance of peace." (*Pastoral Constitution*, #79.)

2. *Conscientious Objection:* "Moreover, it seems just that laws should make humane provision for the case of conscientious objectors who refuse to carry arms, provided they accept some other form of community service." (*Pastoral Constitution*, #79.)

3. *Non-violence:* "In this same spirit we cannot but express our admiration for all who forego the use of violence to vindicate their rights and resort to other means of defense which are available to weaker parties, provided it can be done without harm to the rights

and duties of others and of the community." (*Pastoral Constitution*, #78.)

4. *Citizens and Conscience:* "Once again we deem it opportune to remind our children of their duty to take an active part in public life, and to contribute towards the attainment of the common good of the entire human family as well as to that of their own political community. . . . In other words, it is necessary that human beings, in the intimacy of their own consciences, should so live and act in their temporal lives as to create a synthesis between scientific, technical and professional elements on the one hand, and spiritual values on the other." (Pope John XXIII, *Peace On Earth*, #146, 150.)

II. Moral Principles and Policy Choices

As bishops in the United States, assessing the concrete circumstances of our society, we have made a number of observations and recommendations in the process of applying moral principles to specific policy choices.

A. On the Use of Nuclear Weapons

1. *Counter Population Use:* Under no circumstances may nuclear weapons or other instruments of mass slaughter be used for the purpose of destroying population centers or other predominantly civilian targets. Retaliatory action which would indiscriminately and disproportionately take many wholly innocent lives, lives of people who are in no way responsible for reckless actions of their government, must also be condemned.

2. *The Initiation of Nuclear War:* We do not perceive any situation in which the deliberate initiation of nuclear war, on however restricted a scale, can be morally justified. Non-nuclear attacks by another state must be resisted by other than nuclear means. Therefore, a serious moral obligation exists to develop non-nuclear defensive strategies as rapidly as possible. In this letter we urge NATO to move rapidly toward the adoption of a "no first use" policy, but we recognize this will take time to implement and will require the development of an adequate alternative defense posture.

3. *Limited Nuclear War:* Our examination of the various arguments on this question makes us highly skeptical about the real

meaning of "limited." One of the criteria of the just-war teaching is that there must be a reasonable hope of success in bringing about justice and peace. We must ask whether such a reasonable hope can exist once nuclear weapons have been exchanged. The burden of proof remains on those who assert that meaningful limitation is possible. In our view the first imperative is to prevent any use of nuclear weapons and we hope that leaders will resist the notion that nuclear conflict can be limited, contained or won in any traditional sense.

B. On Deterrence

In concert with the evaluation provided by Pope John Paul II, we have arrived at a strictly conditional moral acceptance of deterrence. In this letter we have outlined criteria and recommendations which indicate the meaning of conditional acceptance of deterrence policy. We cannot consider such a policy adequate as a long-term basis for peace.

C. On Promoting Peace

1. We support immediate, bilateral verifiable agreements to halt the testing, production and deployment of new nuclear weapons systems. This recommendation is not to be identified with any specific political initiative.
2. We support efforts to achieve deep cuts in the arsenals of both superpowers; efforts should concentrate first on systems which threaten the retaliatory forces of either major power.
3. We support early and successful conclusion of negotiations of a comprehensive test ban treaty.
4. We urge new efforts to prevent the spread of nuclear weapons in the world, and to control the conventional arms race, particularly the conventional arms trade.
5. We support, in an increasingly interdependent world, political and economic policies designed to protect human dignity and to promote the human rights of every person, especially the least among us. In this regard, we call for the establishment of some form of global authority adequate to the needs of the international common good.

This letter includes many judgments from the perspective of ethics, politics and strategy needed to speak concretely and correctly to the "moment of supreme crisis" identified by Vatican II. We stress again that readers should be aware, as we have been, of the distinction between our statement of moral principles and of official Church teaching and our application of these to concrete issues. We urge that special care be taken not to use passages out of context; neither should brief portions of this document be cited to support positions it does not intend to convey or which are not truly in accord with the spirit of its teaching.

In concluding this summary we respond to two key questions often asked about this pastoral letter:

Why do we address these matters fraught with such complexity, controversy and passion? We speak as pastors, not politicians. We are teachers, not technicians. We cannot avoid our responsibility to lift up the moral dimensions of the choices before our world and nation. The nuclear age is an era of moral as well as physical danger. We are the first generation since Genesis with the power to threaten the created order. We cannot remain silent in the face of such danger. Why do we address these issues? We are simply trying to live up to the call of Jesus to be peacemakers in our own time and situation.

What are we saying? Fundamentally, we are saying that the decisions about nuclear weapons are among the most pressing moral questions of our age. While these decisions have obvious military and political aspects, they involve fundamental moral choices. In simple terms, we are saying that good ends (defending one's country, protecting freedom, etc.) cannot justify immoral means (the use of weapons which kill indiscriminately and threaten whole societies). We fear that our world and nation are headed in the wrong direction. More weapons with greater destructive potential are produced every day. More and more nations are seeking to become nuclear powers. In our quest for more and more security we fear we are actually becoming less and less secure.

In the words of our Holy Father, we need a "moral about-face." The whole world must summon the moral courage and technical means to say no to nuclear conflict; no to weapons of mass destruction; no to an arms race which robs the poor and the vulnerable; and no to the moral danger of a nuclear age which places before humankind indefensible choices of constant terror or surrender. Peacemaking is not an optional commitment. It is a requirement of our faith. We are called to be peacemakers, not by some movement of the moment, but by our Lord Jesus. The content and context of our peacemaking is set not by some political agenda or ideological program, but by the teaching of his Church.

Ultimately, this letter is intended as an expression of Christian faith, affirming the confidence we have that the risen Lord remains with us precisely in moments of crisis. It is our belief in his presence and power among us which sustain us in confronting the awesome challenge of the nuclear age. We speak from faith to provide hope for all who recognize the challenge and are working to confront it with the resources of faith and reason.

To approach the nuclear issue in faith is to recognize our absolute need for prayer: we urge and invite all to unceasing prayer for peace with justice for all people. In a spirit of prayerful hope we present this message of peace.

INTRODUCTION

1. "The whole human race faces a moment of supreme crisis in its advance toward maturity." Thus the Second Vatican Council opened its treatment of modern warfare.[1] Since the council, the dynamic of the nuclear arms race has intensified. Apprehension about nuclear war is almost tangible and visible today. As Pope John Paul II said in his message to the United Nations concerning disarmament: "Currently, the fear and preoccupation of so many groups in various parts of the world reveals that people are more frightened about what would happen if irresponsible parties unleash some nuclear war."[2]
2. As bishops and pastors ministering in one of the major nuclear nations, we have encountered this terror in the minds and hearts of our people—indeed, we share it. We write this letter because we agree that the world is at a moment of crisis, the effects of which are evident in people's lives. It is not our intent to play on fears, however, but to speak words of hope and encouragement in time of fear. Faith does not insulate us from the challenges of life; rather, it

---

1. Vatican II, the *Pastoral Constitution on the Church in the Modern World* (hereafter cited: *Pastoral Constitution*), #77. Papal and conciliar texts will be referred to by title with paragraph number. Several collections of these texts exist although no single collection is comprehensive; see the following: *Peace and Disarmament: Documents of the World Council of Churches and the Roman Catholic Church* (Geneva and Rome: 1982) (hereafter cited: *Documents*, with page number); J. Gremillion, *The Gospel of Peace and Justice: Catholic Social Teaching Since Pope John* (Maryknoll, N.Y.: 1976); D. J. O'Brien and T. A. Shannon, eds., *Renewing the Earth: Catholic Documents on Peace, Justice and Liberation* (New York: 1977); A. Flannery, O.P., ed., *Vatican Council II: The Conciliar and Post Conciliar Documents* (Collegeville, Minn.: 1975); W. Abbot, ed., *The Documents of Vatican II* (New York: 1966). Both the Flannery and Abbot translations of the *Pastoral Constitution* are used in this letter.

2. John Paul II, "Message to the Second Special Session of the United Nations General Assembly Devoted to Disarmament" (June 1982) (hereafter cited: "Message U.N. Special Session 1982"), #7.

1

intensifies our desire to help solve them precisely in light of the good news which has come to us in the person of Jesus, the Lord of history. From the resources of our faith we wish to provide hope and strength to all who seek a world free of the nuclear threat. Hope sustains one's capacity to live with danger without being overwhelmed by it; hope is the will to struggle against obstacles even when they appear insuperable. Ultimately our hope rests in the God who gave us life, sustains the world by his power, and has called us to revere the lives of every person and all peoples.

3.   The crisis of which we speak arises from this fact: nuclear war threatens the existence of our planet; this is a more menacing threat than any the world has known. It is neither tolerable nor necessary that human beings live under this threat. But removing it will require a major effort of intelligence, courage, and faith. As Pope John Paul II said at Hiroshima: "From now on it is only through a conscious choice and through a deliberate policy that humanity can survive."[3]

4.   As Americans, citizens of the nation which was first to produce atomic weapons, which has been the only one to use them and which today is one of the handful of nations capable of decisively influencing the course of the nuclear age, we have grave human, moral and political responsibilities to see that a "conscious choice" is made to save humanity. This letter is therefore both an invitation and a challenge to Catholics in the United States to join with others in shaping the conscious choices and deliberate policies required in this "moment of supreme crisis."

---

3. John Paul II, "Address to Scientists and Scholars," #4, *Origins* 10 (1981):621.

I. Peace in the Modern World: Religious Perspectives and Principles

5.   The global threat of nuclear war is a central concern of the universal Church, as the words and deeds of recent popes and the Second Vatican Council vividly demonstrate. In this pastoral letter we speak as bishops of the universal Church, heirs of the religious and moral teaching on modern warfare of the last four decades. We also speak as bishops of the Church in the United States, who have both the obligation and the opportunity to share and interpret the moral and religious wisdom of the Catholic tradition by applying it to the problems of war and peace today.

6.   The nuclear threat transcends religious, cultural, and national boundaries. To confront its danger requires all the resources reason and faith can muster. This letter is a contribution to a wider common effort, meant to call Catholics and all members of our political community to dialogue and specific decisions about this awesome question.

7.   The Catholic tradition on war and peace is a long and complex one, reaching from the Sermon on the Mount to the statements of Pope John Paul II. Its development cannot be sketched in a straight line and it seldom gives a simple answer to complex questions. It speaks through many voices and has produced multiple forms of religious witness. As we locate ourselves in this tradition, seeking to draw from it and to develop it, the document which provides profound inspiration and guidance for us is the *Pastoral Constitution on the Church in the Modern World* of Vatican II, for it is based on doctrinal

principles and addresses the relationship of the Church to the world with respect to the most urgent issues of our day.[4]

8. A rule of interpretation crucial for the *Pastoral Constitution* is equally important for this pastoral letter although the authority inherent in these two documents is quite distinct. Both documents use principles of Catholic moral teaching and apply them to specific contemporary issues. The bishops at Vatican II opened the *Pastoral Constitution* with the following guideline on how to relate principles to concrete issues:

> In the first part, the Church develops her teaching on man, on the world which is the enveloping context of man's existence, and on man's relations to his fellow men. In Part II, the Church gives closer consideration to various aspects of modern life and human society; special consideration is given to those questions and problems which, in this general area, seem to have a greater urgency in our day. As a result, in Part II the subject matter which is viewed in the light of doctrinal principles is made up of diverse elements. Some elements have a permanent value; others, only a transitory one. Consequently, the constitution must be interpreted according to the general norms of theological interpretion. Interpreters must bear in mind—especially in Part II—the changeable circumstances which the subject matter, by its very nature, involves.[5]

9. In this pastoral letter, too, we address many concrete questions concerning the arms race, contemporary warfare, weapons systems, and negotiating strategies. We do not intend that our treatment of each of these issues carry the same moral authority as our statement of universal moral principles and formal Church teaching. Indeed, we stress here at the beginning that not every statement in this letter has the same moral authority. At times we reassert universally binding moral principles (e.g., non-combatant immunity and proportionality). At still other times we reaffirm statements of recent popes and the teaching of Vatican II. Again, at other times we apply moral principles to specific cases.

10. When making applications of these principles we realize—and we wish readers to recognize—that prudential judgments are involved based on specific circumstances which can change or which can be interpreted differently by people of good will (e.g., the treat-

---

4. The *Pastoral Constitution* is made up of two parts; yet it constitutes an organic unity. By way of explanation: the constitution is called "pastoral" because, while resting on doctrinal principles, it seeks to express the relation of the Church to the world and modern mankind. The result is that, on the one hand, a pastoral slant is present in the first part and, on the other hand, a doctrinal slant is present in the second part. *Pastoral Constitution*, note 1 above.

5. Ibid.

ment of "no first use"). However, the moral judgments that we make in specific cases, while not binding in conscience, are to be given serious attention and consideration by Catholics as they determine whether their moral judgments are consistent with the Gospel.

11. We shall do our best to indicate, stylistically and substantively, whenever we make such applications. We believe such specific judgments are an important part of this letter, but they should be interpreted in light of another passage from the *Pastoral Constitution*:

> Often enough the Christian view of things will itself suggest some specific solution in certain circumstances. Yet it happens rather frequently, and legitimately so, that with equal sincerity some of the faithful will disagree with others on a given matter. Even against the intention of their proponents, however, solutions proposed on one side or another may be easily confused by many people with the Gospel message. Hence it is necessary for people to remember that no one is allowed in the aforementioned situations to appropriate the Church's authority for his opinion. They should always try to enlighten one another through honest discussion, preserving mutual charity and caring above all for the common good.[6]

12. This passage acknowledges that, on some complex social questions, the Church expects a certain diversity of views even though all hold the same universal moral principles. The experience of preparing this pastoral letter has shown us the range of strongly held opinion in the Catholic community on questions of war and peace. Obviously, as bishops we believe that such differences should be expressed within the framework of Catholic moral teaching. We urge mutual respect among different groups in the Church as they analyze this letter and the issues it addresses. Not only conviction and commitment are needed in the Church, but also civility and charity.

13. The *Pastoral Constitution* calls us to bring the light of the gospel to bear upon "the signs of the times." Three signs of the times have particularly influenced the writing of this letter. The first, to quote Pope John Paul II at the United Nations, is that "the world wants peace, the world needs peace."[7] The second is the judgment of Vatican II about the arms race: "The arms race is one of the greatest curses on the human race and the harm it inflicts upon the poor is more than can be endured."[8] The third is the way in which the unique dangers and dynamics of the nuclear arms race present qualitatively new problems which must be addressed by fresh appli-

---

6. Ibid., #43.

7. John Paul II, "Message U.N. Special Session 1982," #2.

8. *Pastoral Constitution*, #81.

cations of traditional moral principles. In light of these three characteristics, we wish to examine Catholic teaching on peace and war.

14. The Catholic social tradition, as exemplified in the *Pastoral Constitution* and recent papal teachings, is a mix of biblical, theological, and philosophical elements which are brought to bear upon the concrete problems of the day. The biblical vision of the world, created and sustained by God, scarred by sin, redeemed in Christ and destined for the kingdom, is at the heart of our religious heritage. This vision requires elaboration, explanation, and application in each age; the important task of theology is to penetrate ever more adequately the nature of the biblical vision of peace and relate it to a world not yet at peace. Consequently, the teaching about peace examines both how to construct a more peaceful world and how to assess the phenomenon of war.

15. At the center of the Church's teaching on peace and at the center of all Catholic social teaching are the transcendence of God and the dignity of the human person. The human person is the clearest reflection of God's presence in the world; all of the Church's work in pursuit of both justice and peace is designed to protect and promote the dignity of every person. For each person not only reflects God, but is the expression of God's creative work and the meaning of Christ's redemptive ministry. Christians approach the problem of war and peace with fear and reverence. God is the Lord of life, and so each human life is sacred; modern warfare threatens the obliteration of human life on a previously unimaginable scale. The sense of awe and "fear of the Lord" which former generations felt in approaching these issues weighs upon us with new urgency. In the words of the *Pastoral Constitution*:

> Men of this generation should realize that they will have to render an account of their warlike behavior; the destiny of generations to come depends largely on the decisions they make today.[9]

16. Catholic teaching on peace and war has had two purposes: to help Catholics form their consciences and to contribute to the public policy debate about the morality of war. These two purposes have led Catholic teaching to address two distinct but overlapping audiences. The first is the Catholic faithful, formed by the premises of the gospel and the principles of Catholic moral teaching. The second is the wider civil community, a more pluralistic audience, in which our brothers and sisters with whom we share the name Christian, Jews, Moslems, other religious communities, and all people of

---

9. Ibid., #80.

good will also make up our polity. Since Catholic teaching has traditionally sought to address both audiences, we intend to speak to both in this letter, recognizing that Catholics are also members of the wider political community.

17. The conviction, rooted in Catholic ecclesiology, that both the community of the faithful and the civil community should be addressed on peace and war has produced two complementary but distinct styles of teaching. The religious community shares a specific perspective of faith and can be called to live out its implications. The wider civil community, although it does not share the same vision of faith, is equally bound by certain key moral principles. For all men and women find in the depth of their consciences a law written on the human heart by God.[10] From this law reason draws moral norms. These norms do not exhaust the gospel vision, but they speak to critical questions affecting the welfare of the human community, the role of states in international relations, and the limits of acceptable action by individuals and nations on issues of war and peace.

18. Examples of these two styles can be found in recent Catholic teaching. At times the emphasis is upon the problems and requirements for a just public policy (e.g., Pope John Paul II at the U.N. Special Session 1982); at other times the emphasis is on the specific role Christians should play (e.g., Pope John Paul II at Coventry, England, 1982). The same difference of emphasis and orientation can be found in Pope John XXIII's *Peace on Earth* and Vatican II's *Pastoral Constitution.*

19. As bishops we believe that the nature of Catholic moral teaching, the principles of Catholic ecclesiology, and the demands of our pastoral ministry require that this letter speak both to Catholics in a specific way and to the wider political community regarding public policy. Neither audience and neither mode of address can be neglected when the issue has the cosmic dimensions of the nuclear arms race.

20. We propose, therefore, to discuss both the religious vision of peace among peoples and nations and the problems associated with realizing this vision in a world of sovereign states, devoid of any central authority and divided by ideology, geography, and competing claims. We believe the religious vision has an objective basis and is capable of progressive realization. Christ is our peace, for he has "made us both one, and has broken down the dividing wall of hostility . . . that he might create in himself one new man in place of the

---

10. Ibid., #16.

two, so making peace, and might reconcile us both to God" (Eph. 2:14-16). We also know that this peace will be achieved fully only in the kingdom of God. The realization of the kingdom, therefore, is a continuing work, progressively accomplished, precariously maintained, and needing constant effort to preserve the peace achieved and expand its scope in personal and political life.

21. Building peace within and among nations is the work of many individuals and institutions; it is the fruit of ideas and decisions taken in the political, cultural, economic, social, military, and legal sectors of life. We believe that the Church, as a community of faith and social institution, has a proper, necessary, and distinctive part to play in the pursuit of peace.

22. The distinctive contribution of the Church flows from her religious nature and ministry. The Church is called to be, in a unique way, the instrument of the kingdom of God in history. Since peace is one of the signs of that kingdom present in the world, the Church fulfills part of her essential mission by making the peace of the kingdom more visible in our time.

23. Because peace, like the kingdom of God itself, is both a divine gift and a human work, the Church should continually pray for the gift and share in the work. We are called to be a Church at the service of peace, precisely because peace is one manifestation of God's word and work in our midst. Recognition of the Church's responsibility to join with others in the work of peace is a major force behind the call today to develop a theology of peace. Much of the history of Catholic theology on war and peace has focused on limiting the resort to force in human affairs; this task is still necessary, and is reflected later in this pastoral letter, but it is not a sufficient response to Vatican II's challenge "to undertake a completely fresh reappraisal of war." [11]

24. A fresh reappraisal which includes a developed theology of peace will require contributions from several sectors of the Church's life: biblical studies, systematic and moral theology, ecclesiology, and the experience and insights of members of the Church who have struggled in various ways to make and keep the peace in this often violent age. This pastoral letter is more an invitation to continue the new appraisal of war and peace than a final synthesis of the results of such an appraisal. We have some sense of the characteristics of a theology of peace, but not a systematic statement of their relationships.

---

11. Ibid., #80.

8

25.   A theology of peace should ground the task of peacemaking solidly in the biblical vision of the kingdom of God, then place it centrally in the ministry of the Church. It should specify the obstacles in the way of peace, as these are understood theologically and in the social and political sciences. It should both identify the specific contributions a community of faith can make to the work of peace and relate these to the wider work of peace pursued by other groups and institutions in society. Finally, a theology of peace must include a message of hope. The vision of hope must be available to all, but one source of its content should be found in a Church at the service of peace.

26.   We offer now a first step toward a message of peace and hope. It consists of a sketch of the biblical conception of peace; a theological understanding of how peace can be pursued in a world marked by sin; a moral assessment of key issues facing us in the pursuit of peace today; and an assessment of the political and personal tasks required of all people of good will in this most crucial period of history.

A. Peace and the Kingdom

27.   For us as believers, the sacred scriptures provide the foundation for confronting war and peace today. Any use of scripture in this area is conditioned by three factors. *First*, the term "peace" has been understood in different ways at various times and in various contexts. For example, peace can refer to an individual's sense of well-being or security, or it can mean the cessation of armed hostility, producing an atmosphere in which nations can relate to each other and settle conflicts without resorting to the use of arms. For men and women of faith, peace will imply a right relationship with God, which entails forgiveness, reconciliation, and union. Finally, the scriptures point to eschatological peace, a final, full realization of God's salvation when all creation will be made whole. Among these various meanings, the last two predominate in the scriptures and provide direction to the first two.

28.   *Second*, the scriptures as we have them today were written over a long period of time and reflect many varied historical situations, all different from our own. Our understanding of them is both complicated and enhanced by these differences, but not in any way obscured or diminished by them. *Third*, since the scriptures speak

primarily of God's intervention in history, they contain no specific treatise on war and peace. Peace and war must always be seen in light of God's intervention in human affairs and our response to that intervention. Both are elements within the ongoing revelation of God's will for creation.

29. Acknowledging this complexity, we still recognize in the scriptures a unique source of revelation, a word of God which is addressed to us as surely as it has been to all preceding generations. We call upon the spirit of God who speaks in that word and in our hearts to aid us in our listening. The sacred texts have much to say to us about the ways in which God calls us to live in union with and in fidelity to the divine will. They provide us with direction for our lives and hold out to us an object of hope, a final promise, which guides and directs our actions here and now.

1. Old Testament

30. War and peace are significant and highly complex elements within the multilayered accounts of the creation and development of God's people in the Old Testament.

a. War

31. Violence and war are very much present in the history of the people of God, particularly from the Exodus period to the monarchy. God is often seen as the one who leads the Hebrews in battle, protects them from their enemies, makes them victorious over other armies (see, for example, Deut. 1:30; 20:4; Jos. 2:24; Jgs. 3:28). The metaphor of warrior carried multifaceted connotations for a people who knew themselves to be smaller and weaker than the nations which surrounded them. It also enabled them to express their conviction about God's involvement in their lives and his desire for their growth and development. This metaphor provided the people with a sense of security; they had a God who would protect them even in the face of overwhelming obstacles. It was also a call to faith and to trust; the mighty God was to be obeyed and followed. No one can deny the presence of such images in the Old Testament nor their powerful influence upon the articulation of this people's understanding of the involvement of God in their history. The warrior God was highly significant during long periods of Israel's understanding of its faith. But this image was not the only image, and it was gradually transformed, particularly after the experience of the exile, when God was no longer identified with military victory and might. Other

images and other understandings of God's activity became predominant in expressing the faith of God's people.

b. Peace

32. Several points must be taken into account in considering the image of peace in the Old Testament. First, all notions of peace must be understood in light of Israel's relation to God. Peace is always seen as a gift from God and as fruit of God's saving activity. Secondly, the individual's personal peace is not greatly stressed. The well-being and freedom from fear which result from God's love are viewed primarily as they pertain to the community and its unity and harmony. Furthermore, this unity and harmony extend to all of creation; true peace implied a restoration of the right order not just among peoples, but within all of creation. Third, while the images of war and the warrior God become less dominant as a more profound and complex understanding of God is presented in the texts, the images of peace and the demands upon the people for covenantal fidelity to true peace grow more urgent and more developed.

c. Peace and Fidelity to the Covenant

33. If Israel obeyed God's laws, God would dwell among them. "I will walk among you and will be your God and you shall be my people" (Lv. 26:12). God would strengthen the people against those who opposed them and would give peace in the land. The description of life in these circumstances witnesses to unity among peoples and creation, to freedom from fear and to security (Lv. 26:3-16). The right relationship between the people and God was grounded in and expressed by a covenantal union. The covenant bound the people to God in fidelity and obedience; God was also committed in the covenant, to be present with the people, to save them, to lead them to freedom. Peace is a special characteristic of this covenant; when the prophet Ezekiel looked to the establishment of the new, truer covenant, he declared that God would establish an everlasting covenant of peace with the people (Ez. 37:26).

34. Living in covenantal fidelity with God had ramifications in the lives of the people. It was part of fidelity to care for the needy and helpless; a society living with fidelity was one marked by justice and integrity. Furthermore, covenantal fidelity demanded that Israel put its trust in God alone and look only to him for its security. When Israel tended to forget the obligations of the covenant, prophets arose to remind the people and call them to return to God. True peace is an image which they stressed.

35.   Ezekiel, who promised a covenant of peace, condemned in no uncertain terms the false prophets who said there was peace in the land while idolatry and injustice continued (Ez. 13:16). Jeremiah followed in this tradition and berated those who "healed the wounds of the people lightly" and proclaimed peace while injustice and infidelity prevailed (Jer. 6:14; 8:10-12). Jeremiah and Isaiah both condemned the leaders when, against true security, they depended upon their own strength or alliances with other nations rather than trusting in God (Is. 7:1-9; 30:1-4; Jer. 37:10). The lament of Isaiah 48:18 makes clear the connection between justice, fidelity to God's law, and peace; he cries out: "O that you had hearkened to my commandments! Then your peace would have been like a river, and your righteousness like the waves of the sea."

d. Hope for Eschatological Peace

36.   Experience made it clear to the people of God that the covenant of peace and the fullness of salvation had not been realized in their midst. War and enmity were still present, injustices thrived, sin still manifested itself. These same experiences also convinced the people of God's fidelity to a covenant which they often neglected. Because of this fidelity, God's promise of a final salvation involving all peoples and all creation and of an ultimate reign of peace became an integral part of the hope of the Old Testament. In the midst of their failures and sin, God's people strove for greater fidelity to him and closer relationship with him; they did so because, believing in the future they had been promised, they directed their lives and energies toward an eschatological vision for which they longed. Peace is an integral component of that vision.

37.   The final age, the Messianic time, is described as one in which the "Spirit is poured on us from on high." In this age, creation will be made whole, "justice will dwell in the wilderness," the effect of righteousness will be peace, and the people will "abide in a peaceful habitation and in secure dwellings and in quiet resting places" (Is. 32:15-20). There will be no need for instruments of war (Is. 2:4; Mi. 4:3),[12] God will speak directly to the people and "righteousness and peace will embrace each other" (Ps. 85:10-11). A messiah will appear, a servant of God upon whom God has placed his spirit and who will faithfully bring forth justice to the nations: "He will not cry or lift

---

12. The exact opposite of this vision is presented in Joel 3:10 where the foreign nations are told that their weapons will do them no good in the face of God's coming wrath.

up his voice, or make it heard in the street; a bruised reed he will not break and a dimly burning wick he will not quench; he will faithfully bring forth justice." (Is. 42:2-3).

38. The Old Testament provides us with the history of a people who portrayed their God as one who intervened in their lives, who protected them and led them to freedom, often as a mighty leader in battle. They also appear as a people who longed constantly for peace. Such peace was always seen as a result of God's gift which came about in fidelity to the covenantal union. Furthermore, in the midst of their unfulfilled longing, God's people clung tenaciously to hope in the promise of an eschatological time when, in the fullness of salvation, peace and justice would embrace and all creation would be secure from harm. The people looked for a messiah, one whose coming would signal the beginning of that time. In their waiting, they heard the prophets call them to love according to the covenantal vision, to repent, and to be ready for God's reign.

2. New Testament

39. As Christians we believe that Jesus is the messiah or Christ so long awaited. God's servant (Mt. 12:18-21), prophet and more than prophet (Jn. 4:19-26), the one in whom the fullness of God was pleased to dwell, through whom all things in heaven and on earth were reconciled to God, Jesus made peace by the blood of the cross (Col. 1:19-20). While the characteristics of the *shalom* of the Old Testament (gift from God, inclusive of all creation, grounded in salvation and covenantal fidelity, inextricably bound up with justice) are present in the New Testament traditions, all discussion of war and peace in the New Testament must be seen within the context of the unique revelation of God that is Jesus Christ and of the reign of God which Jesus proclaimed and inaugurated.

a. War

40. There is no notion of a warrior God who will lead the people in an historical victory over its enemies in the New Testament. The only war spoken of is found in apocalyptic images of the final moments, especially as they are depicted in the Book of Revelation. Here war stands as image of the eschatological struggle between God and Satan. It is a war in which the Lamb is victorious (Rv. 17:14).

41. Military images appear in terms of the preparedness which one must have for the coming trials (Lk. 14:31; 22:35-38). Swords appear in the New Testament as an image of division (Mt. 12:34;

Heb. 4:12); they are present at the arrest of Jesus, and he rejects their use (Lk. 22:51 and parallel texts); weapons are transformed in Ephesians, when the Christians are urged to put on the whole armor of God which includes the breastplate of righteousness, the helmet of salvation, the sword of the Spirit, "having shod your feet in the equipment of the gospel of peace" (Eph. 6:10-17; cf. I Thes. 5:8-9). Soldiers, too, are present in the New Testament. They are at the crucifixion of Jesus, of course, but they are also recipients of the baptism of John, and one centurion receives the healing of his servant (Mt. 8:5-13 and parallel texts; cf. Jn. 4:46-53).

42. Jesus challenged everyone to recognize in him the presence of the reign of God and to give themselves over to that reign. Such a radical change of allegiance was difficult for many to accept and families found themselves divided, as if by a sword. Hence, the gospels tell us that Jesus said he came not to bring peace but rather the sword (Mt. 10:34). The peace which Jesus did not bring was the false peace which the prophets had warned against. The sword which he did bring was that of the division caused by the word of God which, like a two-edged sword, "pierces to the division of soul and spirit, of joints and marrow, and discerns the thoughts and intentions of the heart" (Heb. 4:12).

43. All are invited into the reign of God. Faith in Jesus and trust in God's mercy are the criteria. Living in accord with the demands of the kingdom rather than those of one's specific profession is decisive.[13]

b. Jesus and Reign of God

44. Jesus proclaimed the reign of God in his words and made it present in his actions. His words begin with a call to conversion and a proclamation of the arrival of the kingdom. "The time is fulfilled, and the kingdom of God is at hand; repent, and believe in the gospel" (Mk. 1:15, Mt. 4:17). The call to conversion was at the same time an invitation to enter God's reign. Jesus went beyond the prophets'

---

13. An omission in the New Testament is significant in this context. Scholars have made us aware of the presence of revolutionary groups in Israel during the time of Jesus. Barabbas, for example, was "among the rebels in prison who had committed murder in the insurrection" (Mk. 15:7). Although Jesus had come to proclaim and to bring about the true reign of God which often stood in opposition to the existing order, he makes no reference to nor does he join in any attempts such as those of the Zealots to overthrow authority by violent means. See M. Smith, "Zealots and Sicarii, Their Origins and Relations," *Harvard Theological Review* 64 (1971):1-19.

cries for conversion when he declared that, in him, the reign of God had begun and was in fact among the people (Lk. 17:20-21; 12:32).

45.   His words, especially as they are preserved for us in the Sermon on the Mount, describe a new reality in which God's power is manifested and the longing of the people is fulfilled. In God's reign the poor are given the kingdom, the mourners are comforted, the meek inherit the earth, those hungry for righteousness are satisfied, the merciful know mercy, the pure see God, the persecuted know the kingdom, and peace-makers are called the children of God (Mt. 5:3-10).

46.   Jesus' words also depict for us the conduct of one who lives under God's reign. His words call for a new way of life which fulfills and goes beyond the law. One of the most striking characteristics of this new way is forgiveness. All who hear Jesus are repeatedly called to forgive one another, and to do so not just once, but many, many times (Mt. 6:14-15; Lk. 6:37; Mt. 18:21-22; Mk. 11:25; Lk. 11:4; 17:3-4). The forgiveness of God, which is the beginning of salvation, is manifested in communal forgiveness and mercy.

47.   Jesus also described God's reign as one in which love is an active, life-giving, inclusive force. He called for a love which went beyond family ties and bonds of friendship to reach even those who were enemies (Mt. 5:44-48; Lk. 6:27-28). Such a love does not seek revenge but rather is merciful in the face of threat and opposition (Mt. 5:39-42; Lk. 6:29-31). Disciples are to love one another as Jesus has loved them (Jn. 15:12).

48.   The words of Jesus would remain an impossible, abstract ideal were it not for two things: the actions of Jesus and his gift of the spirit. In his actions, Jesus showed the way of living in God's reign; he manifested the forgiveness which he called for when he accepted all who came to him, forgave their sins, healed them, released them from the demons who possessed them. In doing these things, he made the tender mercy of God present in a world which knew violence, oppression, and injustice. Jesus pointed out the in-justices of his time and opposed those who laid burdens upon the people or defiled true worship. He acted aggressively and dramatically at times, as when he cleansed the temple of those who had made God's house into a "den of robbers" (Mt. 21:12-17 and parallel texts; Jn. 3:13-25).

49.   Most characteristic of Jesus' actions are those in which he showed his love. As he had commanded others, his love led him even to the giving of his own life to effect redemption. Jesus' message and his actions were dangerous ones in his time, and they led to his death—a cruel and viciously inflicted death, a criminal's death (Gal.

3:13). In all of his suffering, as in all of his life and ministry, Jesus refused to defend himself with force or with violence. He endured violence and cruelty so that God's love might be fully manifest and the world might be reconciled to the One from whom it had become estranged. Even at his death, Jesus cried out for forgiveness for those who were his executioners: "Father, forgive them . . . " (Lk. 23:34).

50. The resurrection of Jesus is the sign to the world that God indeed does reign, does give life in death, and that the love of God is stronger even than death (Rom. 8:36-39).

51. Only in light of this, the fullest demonstration of the power of God's reign, can Jesus' gift of peace—a peace which the world cannot give (Jn. 14:27)—be understood. Jesus gives that peace to his disciples, to those who had witnessed the helplessness of the crucifixion and the power of the resurrection (Jn. 20:19, 20, 26). The peace which he gives to them as he greets them as their risen Lord is the fullness of salvation. It is the reconciliation of the world and God (Rom. 5:1-2; Col. 1:20); the restoration of the unity and harmony of all creation which the Old Testament spoke of with such longing. Because the walls of hostility between God and humankind were broken down in the life and death of the true, perfect servant, union and well-being between God and the world were finally fully possible (Eph. 2:13-22; Gal. 3:28).

c. Jesus and the Community of Believers

52. As his first gift to his followers, the risen Jesus gave his gift of peace. This gift permeated the meetings between the risen Jesus and his followers (Jn. 20:19-29). So intense was that gift and so abiding was its power that the remembrance of that gift and the daily living of it became the hallmark of the community of faith. Simultaneously, Jesus gave his spirit to those who followed him. These two personal and communal gifts are inseparable. In the spirit of Jesus the community of believers was enabled to recognize and to proclaim the savior of the world.

53. Gifted with Jesus' own spirit, they could recognize what God had done and know in their own lives the power of the One who creates from nothing. The early Christian communities knew that this power and the reconciliation and peace which marked it were not yet fully operative in their world. They struggled with external persecution and with interior sin, as do all people. But their experience of the spirit of God and their memory of the Christ who was with them nevertheless enabled them to look forward with unshakable confidence to the time when the fullness of God's reign would make itself known in the world. At the same time, they knew that they were called to be ministers of reconciliation (2 Cor. 5:19-20), people who would make the peace which God had established visible through the love and the unity within their own communities.

54.   Jesus Christ, then, is our peace, and in his death-resurrection he gives God's peace to our world. In him God has indeed reconciled the world, made it one, and has manifested definitively that his will is this reconciliation, this unity between God and all peoples, and among the peoples themselves. The way to union has been opened, the covenant of peace established. The risen Lord's gift of peace is inextricably bound to the call to follow Jesus and to continue the proclamation of God's reign. Matthew's gospel (Mt. 28:16-20; cf. Lk. 24:44-53) tells us that Jesus' last words to his disciples were a sending forth and a promise: "I shall be with you all days." In the continuing presence of Jesus, disciples of all ages find the courage to follow him. To follow Jesus Christ implies continual conversion in one's own life as one seeks to act in ways which are consonant with the justice, forgiveness, and love of God's reign. Discipleship reaches out to the ends of the earth and calls for reconciliation among all peoples so that God's purpose, "a plan for the fullness of time, to unite all things in him" (Eph. 1:10), will be fulfilled.

3. Conclusion

55.   Even a brief examination of war and peace in the scriptures makes it clear that they do not provide us with detailed answers to the specifics of the questions which we face today. They do not speak specifically of nuclear war or nuclear weapons, for these were beyond the imagination of the communities in which the scriptures were formed. The sacred texts do, however, provide us with urgent direction when we look at today's concrete realities. The fullness of eschatological peace remains before us in hope and yet the gift of peace is already ours in the reconciliation effected in Jesus Christ. These two profoundly religious meanings of peace inform and influence all other meanings for Christians. Because we have been gifted with God's peace in the risen Christ, we are called to our own peace and to the making of peace in our world. As disciples and as children of God, it is our task to seek for ways in which to make the forgiveness, justice and mercy and love of God visible in a world where violence and enmity are too often the norm. When we listen to God's word, we hear again and always the call to repentance and to belief: to repentance because although we are redeemed we continue to need

redemption; to belief, because although the reign of God is near, it is still seeking its fullness.

B. Kingdom and History

56. The Christian understanding of history is hopeful and confident but also sober and realistic. "Christian optimism based on the glorious cross of Christ and the outpouring of the Holy Spirit is no excuse for self-deception. For Christians, peace on earth is always a challenge because of the presence of sin in man's heart."[14] Peace must be built on the basis of justice in a world where the personal and social consequences of sin are evident.

57. Christian hope about history is rooted in our belief in God as creator and sustainer of our existence and our conviction that the kingdom of God will come in spite of sin, human weakness, and failure. It is precisely because sin is part of history that the realization of the peace of the kingdom is never permanent or total. This is the continuing refrain from the patristic period to Pope John Paul II:

> For it was sin and hatred that were an obstacle to peace with God and with others: he destroyed them by the offering of life on the cross; he reconciled in one body those who were hostile (cf. Eph. 2:16; Rom. 12:5) . . . Although Christians put all their best energies into preventing war or stopping it, they do not deceive themselves about their ability to cause peace to triumph, nor about the effect of their efforts to this end. They therefore concern themselves with all human initiatives in favor of peace and very often take part in them. But they regard them with realism and humility. One could almost say that they relativize them in two senses: they relate them both to the self-deception of humanity and to God's saving plan.[15]

58. Christians are called to live the tension between the vision of the reign of God and its concrete realization in history. The tension is often described in terms of "already but not yet": i.e., we already live in the grace of the kingdom, but it is not yet the completed kingdom. Hence, we are a pilgrim people in a world marked by conflict and injustice. Christ's grace is at work in the world; his command of love and his call to reconciliation are not purely future ideals but call us to obedience today.

---

14. John Paul II, "World Day of Peace Message 1982," #12, *Origins* 11 (1982): 477.

15. Ibid., #11-12, pp. 477-78.

59. With Pope Paul VI and Pope John Paul II we are convinced that "peace is possible."[16] At the same time, experience convinces us that "in this world a totally and permanently peaceful human society is unfortunately a utopia, and that ideologies that hold up that prospect as easily attainable are based on hopes that cannot be realized, whatever the reason behind them."[17]

60. This recognition—that peace is possible but never assured and that its possibility must be continually protected and preserved in the face of obstacles and attacks upon it—accounts in large measure for the complexity of Catholic teaching on warfare. In the kingdom of God, peace and justice will be fully realized. Justice is always the foundation of peace. In history, efforts to pursue both peace and justice are at times in tension, and the struggle for justice may threaten certain forms of peace.

61. It is within this tension of kingdom and history that Catholic teaching has addressed the problem of war. Wars mark the fabric of human history, distort the life of nations today, and, in the form of nuclear weapons, threaten the destruction of the world as we know it and the civilization which has been patiently constructed over centuries. The causes of war are multiple and not easily identified. Christians will find in any violent situation the consequences of sin: not only sinful patterns of domination, oppression or aggression, but the conflict of values and interests which illustrate the limitations of a sinful world. The threat of nuclear war which affects the world today reflects such sinful patterns and conflicts.

62. In the "already but not yet" of Christian existence, members of the Church choose different paths to move toward the realization of the kingdom in history. As we examine both the positions open to individuals for forming their consciences on war and peace and the Catholic teaching on the obligation of the state to defend society, we draw extensively on the *Pastoral Constitution* for two reasons.

63. First, we find its treatment of the nature of peace and the avoidance of war compelling, for it represents the prayerful thinking of bishops of the entire world and calls vigorously for fresh new attitudes, while faithfully reflecting traditional Church teaching. Secondly, the council fathers were familiar with more than the horrors of World Wars I and II. They saw conflicts continuing "to produce

---

16. John Paul II, "Message U.N. Special Session 1982," #13; Pope Paul VI, "World Day of Peace Message 1973."

17. John Paul II, "World Day of Peace Message 1982," #12, cited, p. 478.

their devastating effect day by day somewhere in the world," the increasing ferocity of warfare made possible by modern scientific weapons, guerrilla warfare "drawn out by new methods of deceit and subversion," and terrorism regarded as a new way to wage war.[18] The same phenomena mark our day.

64. For similar reasons we draw heavily upon the popes of the nuclear age, from Pope Pius XII through Pope John Paul II. The teaching of popes and councils must be incarnated by each local church in a manner understandable to its culture. This allows each local church to bring its unique insights and experience to bear on the issues shaping our world. From 1966 to the present, American bishops, individually and collectively, have issued numerous statements on the issues of peace and war, ranging from the Vietnam War to conscientious objection and the use of nuclear weapons. These statements reflect not only the concerns of the hierarchy but also the voices of our people who have increasingly expressed to us their alarm over the threat of war. In this letter we wish to continue and develop the teaching on peace and war which we have previously made, and which reflects both the teaching of the universal Church and the insights and experience of the Catholic community of the United States.

65. It is significant that explicit treatment of war and peace is reserved for the final chapter of the *Pastoral Constitution.* Only after exploring the nature and destiny of the human person does the council take up the nature of peace, which it sees not as an end in itself, but as an *indispensable condition* for the task "of constructing for all men everywhere a world more genuinely human."[19] An understanding of this task is crucial to understanding the Church's view of the moral choices open to us as Christians.

C. The Moral Choices for the Kingdom

66. In one of its most frequently quoted passages, the *Pastoral Constitution* declares that it is necessary "to undertake a completely fresh reappraisal of war."[20] The council's teaching situates this call for a "fresh reappraisal" within the context of a broad analysis of

---

18. *Pastoral Constitution*, #79.

19. Ibid., #77.

20. Ibid., #80.

the dignity of the human person and the state of the world today. If we lose sight of this broader discussion we cannot grasp the council's wisdom. For the issue of war and peace confronts everyone with a basic question: what contributes to, and what impedes, the construction of a more genuinely human world? If we are to evaluate war with an entirely new attitude, we must be serious about approaching the human person with an entirely new attitude. The obligation for all of humanity to work toward universal respect for human rights and human dignity is a fundamental imperative of the social, economic, and political order.

67.   It is clear, then, that to evaluate war with a new attitude, we must go far beyond an examination of weapons systems or military strategies. We must probe the meaning of the moral choices which are ours as Christians. In accord with the vision of Vatican II, we need to be sensitive to both the danger of war and the conditions of true freedom within which moral choices can be made.[21] Peace is the setting in which moral choice can be most effectively exercised. How can we move toward that peace which is indispensable for true human freedom? How do we define such peace?

1. The Nature of Peace

68.   The Catholic tradition has always understood the meaning of peace in positive terms. Peace is both a gift of God and a human work. It must be constructed on the basis of central human values: truth, justice, freedom, and love. The *Pastoral Constitution* states the traditional conception of peace:

> Peace is not merely the absence of war. Nor can it be reduced solely to the maintenance of a balance of power between enemies. Nor is it brought about by dictatorship. Instead, it is rightly and appropriately called "an enterprise of justice" (Is. 32:17). Peace results from that harmony built into human society by its divine founder and actualized by men as they thirst after ever greater justice.[22]

69.   Pope John Paul II has enhanced this positive conception of peace by relating it with new philosophical depth to the Church's teaching on human dignity and human rights. The relationship was articulated in his 1979 Address to the General Assembly of the United Nations and also in his "World Day of Peace Message 1982":

---

21. Ibid., #17.

22. Ibid., #78.

Unconditional and effective respect for each one's unprescriptable and inalienable rights is the necessary condition in order that peace may reign in a society. Vis-a-vis these basic rights all others are in a way derivatory and secondary. In a society in which these rights are not protected, the very idea of universality is dead, as soon as a small group of individuals set up for their own exclusive advantage a principle of discrimination whereby the rights and even the lives of others are made dependent on the whim of the stronger.[23]

70.   As we have already noted, however, the protection of human rights and the preservation of peace are tasks to be accomplished in a world marked by sin and conflict of various kinds. The Church's teaching on war and peace establishes a strong presumption against war which is binding on all; it then examines when this presumption may be overriden, precisely in the name of preserving the kind of peace which protects human dignity and human rights.

2. The Presumption against War and the Principle of Legitimate Self-Defense

71.   Under the rubric, "curbing the savagery of war," the council contemplates the "melancholy state of humanity." It looks at this world as it is, not simply as we would want it to be. The view is stark: ferocious new means of warfare threatening savagery surpassing that of the past, deceit, subversion, terrorism, genocide. This last crime, in particular, is vehemently condemned as horrendous, but all activities which deliberately conflict with the all-embracing principles of universal natural law, which is permanently binding, are criminal, as are all orders commanding such action. Supreme commendation is due the courage of those who openly and fearlessly resist those who issue such commands. All individuals, especially government officials and experts, are bound to honor and improve upon agreements which are "aimed at making military activity and its consequences less inhuman" and which "better and more workably lead to restraining the frightfulness of war."[24]

72.   This remains a realistic appraisal of the world today. Later in this section the council calls for us "to strain every muscle as we work for the time when all war can be completely outlawed by in-

---

23. John Paul II, "World Day of Peace Message 1982," #9, cited. The *Pastoral Constitution* stresses that peace is not only the fruit of justice, but also love, which commits us to engage in "the studied practice of brotherhood" (#78).

24. *Pastoral Constitution*, #79.

ternational consent." We are told, however, that this goal requires the establishment of some universally recognized public authority with effective power "to safeguard, on the behalf of all, security, regard for justice, and respect for rights."[25] *But what of the present?* The council is exceedingly clear, as are the popes:

> Certainly, war has not been rooted out of human affairs. As long as the danger of war remains and there is no competent and sufficiently powerful authority at the international level, governments cannot be denied the right to legitimate defense once every means of peaceful settlement has been exhausted. Therefore, government authorities and others who share public responsibility have the duty to protect the welfare of the people entrusted to their care and to conduct such grave matters soberly.
>
> But it is one thing to undertake military action for the just defense of the people, and something else again to seek the subjugation of other nations. Nor does the possession of war potential make every military or political use of it lawful. Neither does the mere fact that war has unhappily begun mean that all is fair between the warring parties.[26]

73.   The Christian has no choice but to defend peace, properly understood, against aggression. This is an inalienable obligation. It is the *how* of defending peace which offers moral options. We stress this principle again because we observe so much misunderstanding about both those who resist bearing arms and those who bear them. Great numbers from both traditions provide examples of exceptional courage, examples the world continues to need. Of the millions of men and women who have served with integrity in the armed forces, many have laid down their lives. Many others serve today throughout the world in the difficult and demanding task of helping to preserve that "peace of a sort" of which the council speaks. We see many deeply sincere individuals who, far from being indifferent or apathetic to world evils, believe strongly in conscience that they are best defending true peace by refusing to bear arms. In some cases they are motivated by their understanding of the gospel and the life and death of Jesus as forbidding all violence. In others, their motivation is simply to give personal example of Christian forbearance as a positive, constructive approach toward loving reconciliation with enemies. In still other cases, they propose or engage in "active non-violence" as programmed resistance to thwart aggression, or to render ineffective any oppression attempted by force of arms. No government, and

---

25. Ibid., #82.
26. Ibid., #79.

certainly no Christian, may simply assume that such individuals are mere pawns of conspiratorial forces or guilty of cowardice.

74. Catholic teaching sees these two distinct moral responses as having a complementary relationship, in the sense that both seek to serve the common good. They differ in their perception of how the common good is to be defended most effectively, but both responses testify to the Christian conviction that peace must be pursued and rights defended within moral restraints and in the context of defining other basic human values.

75. In all of this discussion of distinct choices, of course, we are referring to options open to individuals. The council and the popes have stated clearly that governments threatened by armed, unjust aggression must defend their people. This includes defense by armed force if necessary as a last resort. We shall discuss below the conditions and limits imposed on such defense. Even when speaking of individuals, however, the council is careful to preserve the fundamental *right* of defense. Some choose not to vindicate their rights by armed force and adopt other methods of defense, but they do not lose the right of defense nor may they renounce their obligations to others. They are praised by the council, as long as the rights and duties of others or of the community itself are not injured.

76. Pope Pius XII is especially strong in his conviction about the responsibility of the Christian to resist unjust aggression:

> *A people threatened with an unjust aggression, or already its victim, may not remain passively indifferent, if it would think and act as befits a Christian.* All the more does the solidarity of the family of nations forbid others to behave as mere spectators, in any attitude of apathetic neutrality. Who will ever measure the harm already caused in the past by such indifference to war of aggression, which is quite alien to the Christian instinct? How much more keenly has it brought any advantage in recompense? On the contrary, it has only reassured and encouraged the authors and fomentors of aggression, while it obliges the several peoples, left to themselves, to increase their armaments indefinitely . . . Among (the) goods (of humanity) some are of such importance for society, that it is perfectly lawful to defend them against unjust aggression. *Their defense is even an obligation for the nations as a whole, who have a duty not to abandon a nation that is attacked.*[27]

---

27. Pius XII, "Christmas Message," 1948; The same theme is reiterated in Pius XII's "Message" of October 3, 1953: "The community of nations must reckon with unprincipled criminals who, in order to realize their ambitious plans, are not afraid to unleash total war. This is the reason why other countries if they wish to preserve their very existence and their most precious possessions, and unless they are prepared to accord free action to international criminals, have no alternative but to get ready for the day when they must defend themselves. *This right to be prepared for self-defense cannot be denied, even in these days, to any state.*"

77.   None of the above is to suggest, however, that armed force is the only defense against unjust aggression, regardless of circumstances. Well does the council require that grave matters concerning the protection of peoples be conducted *soberly*. The council fathers were well aware that in today's world, the "horror and perversity of war are immensely magnified by the multiplication of scientific weapons. For acts of war involving these weapons can inflict massive and indiscriminate destruction far exceeding the bounds of legitimate defense."[28] Hence, we are warned: "Men of our time must realize that they will have to give a somber reckoning for their deeds of war. For the course of the future will depend largely on the decisions they make today."[29] There must be serious and continuing study and efforts to develop programmed methods for both individuals and nations to defend against unjust aggression without using violence.

78.   We believe work to develop non-violent means of fending off aggression and resolving conflict best reflects the call of Jesus both to love and to justice. Indeed, each increase in the potential destructiveness of weapons and therefore of war serves to underline the rightness of the way that Jesus mandated to his followers. But, on the other hand, the fact of aggression, oppression and injustice in our world also serves to legitimate the resort to weapons and armed force in defense of justice. We must recognize the reality of the paradox we face as Christians living in the context of the world as it presently exists, we must continue to articulate our belief that love is possible and the only real hope for all human relations, and yet accept that force, even deadly force, is sometimes justified and that nations must provide for their defense. It is the mandate of Christians, in the face of this paradox, to strive to resolve it through an even greater commitment to Christ and his message. As Pope John Paul II said:

> Christians are aware that plans based on aggression, domination and the manipulation of others lurk in human hearts, and sometimes even secretly nourish human intentions, in spite of certain declarations or manifestations of a pacifist nature. For Christians know that in this world a totally and permanently peaceful human society is unfortunately a utopia, and that ideologies that hold up that prospect as easily attainable are based on hopes that cannot be realized, whatever the reason behind them. It is a question of a mistaken view of the human condition, a lack of application in considering the question as a whole; or it may be a case of evasion in order to calm fear, or in still other cases a matter of calculated self-interest.

---

28. *Pastoral Constitution*, #80.

29. Ibid.

Christians are convinced, if only because they have learned from personal experience, that these deceptive hopes lead straight to the false peace of totalitarian regimes. But this realistic view in no way prevents Christians from working for peace; instead, it stirs up their ardor, for they also know that Christ's victory over deception, hate and death gives those in love with peace a more decisive motive for action than what the most generous theories about man have to offer; Christ's victory likewise gives a hope more surely based than any hope held out by the most audacious dreams.

This is why Christians, even as they strive to resist and prevent every form of warfare, have no hesitation in recalling that, in the name of an elementary requirement of justice, peoples have a right and even a duty to protect their existence and freedom by proportionate means against an unjust aggressor.[30]

79.   In light of the framework of Catholic teaching on the nature of peace, the avoidance of war, and the state's right of legitimate defense, we can now spell out certain moral principles within the Catholic tradition which provide guidance for public policy and individual choice.

3. The Just-War Criteria

80.   The moral theory of the "just-war" or "limited-war" doctrine begins with the presumption which binds all Christians: we should do no harm to our neighbors; how we treat our enemy is the key test of whether we love our neighbor; and the possibility of taking even one human life is a prospect we should consider in fear and trembling. How is it possible to move from these presumptions to the idea of a justifiable use of lethal force?

81.   Historically and theologically the clearest answer to the question is found in St. Augustine. Augustine was impressed by the fact and the consequences of sin in history—the "not yet" dimension of the kingdom. In his view war was both the result of sin and a tragic remedy for sin in the life of political societies. War arose from disordered ambitions, but it could also be used, in some cases at least, to restrain evil and protect the innocent. The classic case which illustrated his view was the use of lethal force to prevent aggression against innocent victims. Faced with the fact of attack on the innocent, the presumption that we do no harm, even to our enemy, yielded to the command of love understood as the need to restrain an enemy who would injure the innocent.

---

30. John Paul II, "World Day of Peace Message 1982," #12, cited, p. 478.

26

82. The just-war argument has taken several forms in the history of Catholic theology, but this Augustinian insight is its central premise.[31] In the twentieth century, papal teaching has used the logic of Augustine and Aquinas[32] to articulate a right of self-defense for states in a decentralized international order and to state the criteria for exercising that right. The essential position was stated by Vatican II: "As long as the danger of war persists and there is no international authority with the necessary competence and power, governments cannot be denied the right of lawful self-defense, once all peace efforts have failed."[33] We have already indicated the centrality of this principle for understanding Catholic teaching about the state and its duties.

83. Just-war teaching has evolved, however, as an effort to prevent war; only if war cannot be rationally avoided, does the teaching then seek to restrict and reduce its horrors. It does this by establishing a set of rigorous conditions which must be met if the decision to go to war is to be morally permissible. Such a decision, especially today, requires extraordinarily strong reasons for overriding the presumption *in favor of peace* and *against* war. This is one significant reason why valid just-war teaching makes provision for conscientious dissent. It is presumed that all sane people prefer peace, never *want* to initiate war, and accept even the most justifiable defensive war only as a sad necessity. Only the most powerful reasons may be permitted to override such objection. In the words of Pope Pius XII:

> The Christian will for peace . . . is very careful to avoid recourse to the force of arms in the defense of rights which, however legitimate, do not offset the risk of kindling a blaze with all its spiritual and material consequences.[34]

---

31. Augustine called it a Manichaean heresy to assert that war is intrinsically evil and contrary to Christian charity, and stated: "War and conquest are a sad necessity in the eyes of men of principle, yet it would be still more unfortunate if wrongdoers should dominate just men." (*The City of God*, Book IV, C. 15)

Representative surveys of the history and theology of the just-war tradition include: F. H. Russell, *The Just War in the Middle Ages* (New York: 1975); P. Ramsey, *War and the Christian Conscience* (Durham, N.C.: 1961); P. Ramsey, *The Just War: Force and Political Responsibility* (New York: 1968), James T. Johnson, *Ideology, Reason and the Limitation of War* (Princeton: 1975), *Just War Tradition and the Restraint of War: A Moral and Historical Inquiry* (Princeton: 1981); L. B. Walters, *Five Classic Just-War Theories* (Ph.D. Dissertation, Yale University, 1971); W. O'Brien, *War and/or Survival* (New York: 1969), *The Conduct of Just and Limited War* (New York: 1981); J. C. Murray, "Remarks on the Moral Problem of War," *Theological Studies* 20 (1959):40-61.

32. Aquinas treats the question of war in the *Summa Theologica*, II-IIae, q. 40; also cf. II-IIae, q. 64.

33. *Pastoral Constitution*, #79.

34. Pius XII, "Christmas Message," 1948.

84. The determination of *when* conditions exist which allow the resort to force in spite of the strong presumption against it is made in light of *jus ad bellum* criteria. The determination of *how* even a justified resort to force must be conducted is made in light of the *jus in bello* criteria. We shall briefly explore the meaning of both.[35]

Jus ad Bellum

85. Why and when recourse to war is permissible.

86. *a) Just Cause:* War is permissible only to confront "a real and certain danger," i.e., to protect innocent life, to preserve conditions necessary for decent human existence, and to secure basic human rights. As both Pope Pius XII and Pope John XXIII made clear, if war of retribution was ever justifiable, the risks of modern war negate such a claim today.

87. *b) Competent Authority:* In the Catholic tradition the right to use force has always been joined to the common good; war must be declared by those with responsibility for public order, not by private groups or individuals.

88. The requirement that a decision to go to war must be made by competent authority is particularly important in a democratic society. It needs detailed treatment here since it involves a broad spectrum of related issues. Some of the bitterest divisions of society in our own nation's history, for example, have been provoked over the question of whether or not a president of the United States has acted constitutionally and legally in involving our country in a *de facto* war, even if—indeed, especially if—war was never formally declared. Equally perplexing problems of conscience can be raised for individuals expected or legally required to go to war even though our duly elected representatives in Congress have, in fact, voted for war.

89. The criterion of competent authority is of further importance in a day when revolutionary war has become commonplace. Historically, the just-war tradition has been open to a "just revolution" position, recognizing that an oppressive government may lose its claim to legitimacy. Insufficient analytical attention has been given to the moral issues of revolutionary warfare. The mere possession of sufficient weaponry, for example, does not legitimize the initiation of war by "insurgents" against an established government, any more

---

35. For an analysis of the content and relationship of these principles cf.: R. Potter, "The Moral Logic of War," *McCormick Quarterly* 23 (1970):203-33; J. Childress, "Just War Criteria," in T. Shannon, ed., *War or Peace: The Search for New Answers* (N.Y.: 1980).

than the government's systematic oppression of its people can be carried out under the doctrine of "national security."

90.   While the legitimacy of revolution in some circumstances cannot be denied, just-war teachings must be applied as rigorously to revolutionary-counterrevolutionary conflicts as to others. The issue of who constitutes competent authority and how such authority is exercised is essential.

91.   When we consider in this letter the issues of conscientious objection (C.O.) and selective conscientious objection (S.C.O.), the issue of competent authority will arise again.

92.   *c) Comparative Justice:* Questions concerning the *means* of waging war today, particularly in view of the destructive potential of weapons, have tended to override questions concerning the comparative justice of the positions of respective adversaries or enemies. In essence: which side is sufficiently "right" in a dispute, and are the values at stake critical enough to override the presumption against war? The question in its most basic form is this: do the rights and values involved justify killing? For whatever the means used, war, by definition, involves violence, destruction, suffering, and death.

93.   The category of comparative justice is designed to emphasize the presumption against war which stands at the beginning of just-war teaching. In a world of sovereign states recognizing neither a common moral authority nor a central political authority, comparative justice stresses that no state should act on the basis that it has "absolute justice" on its side. Every party to a conflict should acknowledge the limits of its "just cause" and the consequent requirement to use *only* limited means in pursuit of its objectives. Far from legitimizing a crusade mentality, comparative justice is designed to relativize absolute claims and to restrain the use of force even in a "justified" conflict.[36]

94.   Given techniques of propaganda and the ease with which nations and individuals either assume or delude themselves into believing that God or right is clearly on their side, the test of comparative justice may be extremely difficult to apply. Clearly, however, this is not the case in every instance of war. Blatant aggression from without

---

36. James T. Johnson, *Ideology, Reason and the Limitation of War*, cited; W. O'Brien, *The Conduct of Just and Limited War*, cited, pp. 13-30; W. Vanderpol, *La doctrine scolastique du droit de guerre*, p. 387ff; J. C. Murray, "Theology and Modern Warfare," in W. J. Nagel, ed., *Morality and Modern Warfare*, p. 80ff.

and subversion from within are often enough readily identifiable by all reasonably fair-minded people.

95.   *d) Right Intention:* Right intention is related to just cause—war can be legitimately intended only for the reasons set forth above as a just cause. During the conflict, right intention means pursuit of peace and reconciliation, including avoiding unnecessarily destructive acts or imposing unreasonable conditions (e.g., unconditional surrender).

96.   *e) Last Resort:* For resort to war to be justified, all peaceful alternatives must have been exhausted. There are formidable problems in this requirement. No international organization currently in existence has exercised sufficient internationally recognized authority to be able either to mediate effectively in most cases or to prevent conflict by the intervention of United Nations or other peacekeeping forces. Furthermore, there is a tendency for nations or peoples which perceive conflict between or among other nations as advantageous to themselves to attempt to prevent a peaceful settlement rather than advance it.

97.   We regret the apparent unwillingness of some to see in the United Nations organization the potential for world order which exists and to encourage its development. Pope Paul VI called the United Nations the last hope for peace. The loss of this hope cannot be allowed to happen. Pope John Paul II is again instructive on this point:

> I wish above all to repeat my confidence in you, the leaders and members of the International Organizations, and in you, the international officials! In the course of the last ten years, your organizations have too often been the object of attempts at manipulation on the part of nations wishing to exploit such bodies. However it remains true that the present multiplicity of violent clashes, divisions and blocks on which bilateral relations founder, offer the great International Organizations the opportunity to engage upon the qualitative change in their activities, even to reform on certain points their own structures in order to take into account new realities and to enjoy effective power.[37]

98.   *f) Probability of Success:* This is a difficult criterion to apply, but its purpose is to prevent irrational resort to force or hopeless resistance when the outcome of either will clearly be disproportionate or futile. The determination includes a recognition that at times defense of key values, even against great odds, may be a "proportionate" witness.

---

37. John Paul II, "World Day of Peace Message 1983," #11.

99.   *g) **Proportionality:*** In terms of the *jus ad bellum* criteria, proportionality means that the damage to be inflicted and the costs incurred by war must be proportionate to the good expected by taking up arms. Nor should judgments concerning proportionality be limited to the temporal order without regard to a spiritual dimension in terms of "damage," "cost," and "the good expected." In today's interdependent world even a local conflict can affect people everywhere; this is particularly the case when the nuclear powers are involved. Hence a nation cannot justly go to war today without considering the effect of its action on others and on the international community.

100.   This principle of proportionality applies throughout the conduct of the war as well as to the decision to begin warfare. During the Vietnam war our bishops' conference ultimately concluded that the conflict had reached such a level of devastation to the adversary and damage to our own society that continuing it could not be justified.[38]

Jus in Bello

101.   Even when the stringent conditions which justify resort to war are met, the conduct of war (i.e., strategy, tactics, and individual actions) remains subject to continuous scrutiny in light of two principles which have special significance today precisely because of the destructive capability of modern technological warfare. These principles are proportionality and discrimination. In discussing them here, we shall apply them to the question of *jus ad bellum* as well as *jus in bello*; for today it becomes increasingly difficult to make a decision to use any kind of armed force, however limited initially in intention and in the destructive power of the weapons employed, without facing at least the possibility of escalation to broader, or even total, war and to the use of weapons of horrendous destructive potential. This is especially the case when adversaries are "superpowers," as the council clearly envisioned:

> Indeed, if the kind of weapons now stocked in the arsenals of the great powers were to be employed to the fullest, the result would be the almost complete reciprocal slaughter of one side by the other, not to speak of the widespread devastation that would follow in the world and the deadly after-effects resulting from the use of such weapons.[39]

---

38. National Conference of Catholic Bishops, *Resolution on Southeast Asia* (Washington, D.C.: 1971).

39. *Pastoral Constitution*, #80.

102.   It should not be thought, of course, that massive slaughter and destruction would result only from the extensive use of nuclear weapons. We recall with horror the carpet and incendiary bombings of World War II, the deaths of hundreds of thousands in various regions of the world through "conventional" arms, the unspeakable use of gas and other forms of chemical warfare, the destruction of homes and of crops, the utter suffering war has wrought during the centuries before and the decades since the use of the "atom bomb." Nevertheless, every honest person must recognize that, especially given the proliferation of modern scientific weapons, we now face possibilities which are appalling to contemplate. Today, as never before, we must ask not merely what *will* happen, but what *may* happen, especially if major powers embark on war. Pope John Paul II has repeatedly pleaded that world leaders confront this reality:

> [I]n view of the difference between classical warfare and nuclear or bacteriological war—a difference so to speak of nature—and in view of the scandal of the arms race seen against the background of the needs of the Third World, this right [of defense], which is very real in principle, only underlines the urgency of world society to equip itself with effective means of negotiation. In this way the nuclear terror that haunts our time can encourage us to enrich our common heritage with a very simple discovery that is within our reach, namely that war is the most barbarous and least effective way of resolving conflicts.[40]

103.   The Pontifical Academy of Sciences reaffirmed the Holy Father's theme, in its November 1981 "Statement on the Consequences of Nuclear War." Then, in a meeting convoked by the Pontifical Academy, representatives of national academies of science from throughout the world issued a "Declaration on the Prevention of Nuclear War" which specified the meaning of Pope John Paul II's statement that modern warfare differs by nature from previous forms of war. The scientists said:

> Throughout its history humanity has been confronted with war, but since 1945 the nature of warfare has changed so profoundly that the future of the human race, of generations yet unborn, is imperiled. . . . For the first time it is possible to cause damage on such a catastrophic scale as to wipe out a large part of civilization and to endanger its very survival. The large-scale use of such weapons could trigger major and irreversible ecological and genetic changes whose limits cannot be predicted.[41]

And earlier, with such thoughts plainly in mind, the council had

---

40. John Paul II, "World Day of Peace Message 1982," #12, cited.

41. "Declaration on Prevention of Nuclear War" (Sept. 24, 1982).

made its own "the condemnation of total war already pronounced by recent popes."[42] This condemnation is demanded by the principles of proportionality and discrimination. Response to aggression must not exceed the nature of the aggression. To destroy civilization as we know it by waging a "total war" as today it *could* be waged would be a monstrously disproportionate response to aggression on the part of any nation.

104. Moreover, the lives of innocent persons may never be taken directly, regardless of the purpose alleged for doing so. To wage truly "total" war is by definition to take huge numbers of innocent lives. Just response to aggression must be discriminate; it must be directed against unjust aggressors, not against innocent people caught up in a war not of their making. The council therefore issued its memorable declaration:

> Any act of war aimed indiscriminately at the destruction of entire cities or of extensive areas along with their population is a crime against God and man himself. It merits unequivocal and unhesitating condemnation.[43]

105. When confronting choices among specific military options, the question asked by proportionality is: once we take into account not only the military advantages that will be achieved by using this means but also all the harms reasonably expected to follow from using it, can its use still be justified? We know, of course, that no end can justify means evil in themselves, such as the executing of hostages or the targeting of non-combatants. Nonetheless, even if the means adopted is not evil in itself, it is necessary to take into account the probable harms that will result from using it and the justice of accepting those harms. It is of utmost importance, in assessing harms and the justice of accepting them, to think about the poor and the helpless, for they are usually the ones who have the least to gain and the most to lose when war's violence touches their lives.

106. In terms of the arms race, if the *real* end in view is legitimate defense against unjust aggression, and the means to this end are not evil in themselves, we must still examine the question of proportionality concerning attendant evils. Do the exorbitant costs, the general climate of insecurity generated, the possibility of accidental detonation of highly destructive weapons, the danger of error and miscalculation that could provoke retaliation and war—do such evils or others attendant upon and indirectly deriving from the arms race

---

42. *Pastoral Constitution*, #80.

43. Ibid.

make the arms race itself a disproportionate response to aggression? Pope John Paul II is very clear in his insistence that the exercise of the right and duty of a people to protect their existence and freedom is contingent on the use of proportionate means.[44]

107. Finally, another set of questions concerns the interpretation of the principle of discrimination. The principle prohibits directly intended attacks on non-combatants and non-military targets. It raises a series of questions about the term "intentional," the category of "non-combatant," and the meaning of "military."

108. These questions merit the debate occurring with increasing frequency today. We encourage such debate, for concise and definitive answers still appear to be wanting. Mobilization of forces in modern war includes not only the military, but to a significant degree the political, economic, and social sectors. It is not always easy to determine who is directly involved in a "war effort" or to what degree. Plainly, though, not even by the broadest definition can one rationally consider combatants entire classes of human beings such as schoolchildren, hospital patients, the elderly, the ill, the average industrial worker producing goods not directly related to military purposes, farmers, and many others. They may never be directly attacked.

109. Direct attacks on military targets involve similar complexities. Which targets are "military" ones and which are not? To what degree, for instance, does the use (by either revolutionaries or regular military forces) of a village or housing in a civilian populated area invite attack? What of a munitions factory in the heart of a city? Who is directly responsible for the deaths of noncombatants should the attack be carried out? To revert to the question raised earlier, how many deaths of non-combatants are "tolerable" as a result of indirect attacks—attacks directed against combat forces and military targets, which nevertheless kill non-combatants at the same time?

110. These two principles, in all their complexity, must be applied to the range of weapons—conventional, nuclear, biological, and chemical—with which nations are armed today.

4. The Value of Non-violence

111. Moved by the example of Jesus' life and by his teaching, some Christians have from the earliest days of the Church committed

---

44. John Paul II, "World Day of Peace Message 1982," #12, cited.

themselves to a non-violent lifestyle.[45] Some understood the gospel of Jesus to prohibit all killing. Some affirmed the use of prayer and other spiritual methods as means of responding to enmity and hostility.

112. In the middle of the second century, St. Justin proclaimed to his pagan readers that Isaiah's prophecy about turning swords into ploughshares and spears into sickles had been fulfilled as a consequence of Christ's coming:

> And we who delighted in war, in the slaughter of one another, and in every other kind of iniquity have in every part of the world converted our weapons into implements of peace—our swords into ploughshares, our spears into farmers' tools—and we cultivate piety, justice, brotherly charity, faith and hope, which we derive from the Father through the crucified Savior . . .[46]

113. Writing in the third century, St. Cyprian of Carthage struck a similar note when he indicated that the Christians of his day did not fight against their enemies. He himself regarded their conduct as proper:

> They do not even fight against those who are attacking since it is not granted to the innocent to kill even the aggressor, but promptly to deliver up their souls and blood that, since so much malice and cruelty are rampant in the world, they may more quickly withdraw from the malicious and the cruel.[47]

114. Some of the early Christian opposition to military service was a response to the idolatrous practices which prevailed in the Roman army. Another powerful motive was the fact that army service involved preparation for fighting and killing. We see this in the case of St. Martin of Tours during the fourth century, who renounced his soldierly profession with the explanation: "Hitherto I have served you as a soldier. Allow me now to become a soldier of God . . . I am a soldier of Christ. It is not lawful for me to fight."[48]

---

45. Representative authors in the tradition of Christian pacifism and non-violence include: R. Bainton, *Christian Attitudes Toward War and Peace* (Abington: 1960), chs. 4, 5, 10; J. Yoder, *The Politics of Jesus* (Grand Rapids: 1972), *Nevertheless: Varieties of Religious Pacifism* (Scottsdale: 1971); T. Merton, *Faith and Violence: Christian Teaching and Christian Practice* (Notre Dame: 1968); G. Zahn, *War, Conscience and Dissent* (New York: 1967); E. Egan, "The Beatitudes: Works of Mercy and Pacifism," in T. Shannon, ed., *War or Peace: The Search for New Answers* (New York: 1980), pp. 169-187; J. Fahey, "The Catholic Church and the Arms Race," *Worldview* 22 (1979):38-41; J. Douglass, *The Nonviolent Cross: A Theology of Revolution and Peace* (New York: 1966).

46. Justin, *Dialogue with Trypho*, ch. 110; cf. also *The First Apology*, chs. 14, 39.

47. Cyprian, *Collected Letters*; Letters to Cornelius.

48. Sulpicius Severus, *The Life of Martin*, 4.3.

115.   In the centuries between the fourth century and our own day, the theme of Christian non-violence and Christian pacifism has echoed and re-echoed, sometimes more strongly, sometimes more faintly. One of the great non-violent figures in those centuries was St. Francis of Assisi. Besides making personal efforts on behalf of reconciliation and peace, Francis stipulated that laypersons who became members of his Third Order were not "to take up lethal weapons, or bear them about, against anybody."

116.   The vision of Christian non-violence is not passive about injustice and the defense of the rights of others; it rather affirms and exemplifies what it means to resist injustice through non-violent methods.

117.   In the twentieth century, prescinding from the non-Christian witness of a Mahatma Ghandi and its worldwide impact, the non-violent witness of such figures as Dorothy Day and Martin Luther King has had a profound impact upon the life of the Church in the United States. The witness of numerous Christians who had preceded them over the centuries was affirmed in a remarkable way at the Second Vatican Council.

118.   Two of the passages which were included in the final version of the *Pastoral Constitution* gave particular encouragement for Catholics in all walks of life to assess their attitudes toward war and military service in the light of Christian pacifism. In paragraph 79 the council fathers called upon governments to enact laws protecting the rights of those who adopted the position of conscientious objection to all war: "Moreover, it seems right that laws make humane provisions for the case of those who for reasons of conscience refuse to bear arms, provided, however, that they accept some other form of service to the human community."[49] This was the first time a call for legal protection of conscientious objection had appeared in a document of such prominence. In addition to its own profound meaning this statement took on even more significance in the light of the praise that the council fathers had given in the preceding section "to those who renounce the use of violence and the vindication of their rights."[50] In *Human Life in Our Day* (1968) we called for legislative provision to recognize selective conscientious objectors as well.[51]

---

49. *Pastoral Constitution*, #79.

50. Ibid., #78.

51. United States Catholic Conference, *Human Life in Our Day* (Washington, D.C.: 1968), p. 44.

119.   As Catholic bishops it is incumbent upon us to stress to our own community and to the wider society the significance of this support for a pacifist option for individuals in the teaching of Vatican II and the reaffirmation that the popes have given to nonviolent witness since the time of the council.

120.   In th development of a theology of peace and the growth of the Christian pacifist position among Catholics, these words of the *Pastoral Constitution* have special significance: "All these factors force us to undertake a completely fresh reappraisal of war."[52] The council fathers had reference to "the development of armaments by modern science (which) has immeasurably magified the horrors and wickedness of war."[53] While the just-war teaching has clearly been in possession for the past 1,500 years of Catholic thought, the "new moment" in which we find ourselves sees the just-war teaching and non-violence as distinct but interdependent methods of evaluating warfare. They diverge on some specific conclusions, but they share a common presumption against the use of force as a means of settling disputes.

121.   Both find their roots in the Christian theological tradition; each contributes to the full moral vision we need in pursuit of a human peace. We believe the two perspectives support and complement one another, each preserving the other from distortion. Finally, in an age of technological warfare, analysis from the viewpoint of non-violence and analysis from the viewpoint of the just-war teaching often converge and agree in their opposition to methods of warfare which are in fact indistinguishable from total warfare.

---

52. *Pastoral Constitution*, #80.

53. Ibid.

II. War and Peace in the Modern World: Problems and Principles

122.   Both the just-war teaching and non-violence are confronted with a unique challenge by nuclear warfare. This must be the starting point of any further moral reflection: nuclear weapons particularly and nuclear warfare as it is planned today, raise new moral questions. No previously conceived moral position escapes the fundamental confrontation posed by contemporary nuclear strategy. Many have noted the similarity of the statements made by eminent scientists and Vatican II's observation that we are forced today "to undertake a completely fresh reappraisal of war." The task before us is not simply to repeat what we have said before; it is first to consider anew whether and how our religious-moral tradition can assess, direct, contain, and, we hope, help to eliminate the threat posed to the human family by the nuclear arsenals of the world. Pope John Paul II captured the essence of the problem during his pilgrimage to Hiroshima:

> In the past it was possible to destroy a village, a town, a region, even a country. Now it is the whole planet that has come under threat.[54]

123.   The Holy Father's observation illustrates why the moral problem is also a religious question of the most profound significance. In the nuclear arsenals of the United States or the Soviet Union alone, there exists a capacity to do something no other age could imagine: we can threaten the entire planet.[55] For people of faith this means we read the Book of Genesis with a new awareness; the moral issue at stake in nuclear war involves the meaning of sin in its most graphic dimensions. Every sinful act is a confrontation of the creature and

---

54. John Paul II, "Address to Scientists and Scholars," #4, cited, p. 621.

55. Cf. "Declaration on Prevention of Nuclear War."

the creator. Today the destructive potential of the nuclear powers threatens the human person, the civilization we have slowly constructed, and even the created order itself.

124. We live today, therefore, in the midst of a cosmic drama; we possess a power which should never be used, but which might be used if we do not reverse our direction. We live with nuclear weapons knowing we cannot afford to make one serious mistake. This fact dramatizes the precariousness of our position, politically, morally, and spiritually.

125. A prominent "sign of the times" today is a sharply increased awareness of the danger of the nuclear arms race. Such awareness has produced a public discussion about nuclear policy here and in other countries which is unprecedented in its scope and depth. What has been accepted for years with almost no question is now being subjected to the sharpest criticism. What previously had been defined as a safe and stable system of deterrence is today viewed with political and moral skepticism. Many forces are at work in this new evaluation, and we believe one of the crucial elements is the gospel vision of peace which guides our work in this pastoral letter. The nuclear age has been the theater of our existence for almost four decades; today it is being evaluated with a new perspective. For many the leaven of the gospel and the light of the Holy Spirit create the decisive dimension of this new perspective.

A. The New Moment

126. At the center of the new evaluation of the nuclear arms race is a recognition of two elements: the destructive potential of nuclear weapons, and the stringent choices which the nuclear age poses for both politics and morals.

127. The fateful passage into the nuclear age as a military reality began with the bombing of Nagasaki and Hiroshima, events described by Pope Paul VI as a "butchery of untold magnitude."[56] Since then, in spite of efforts at control and plans for disarmament (e.g., the Baruch Plan of 1946), the nuclear arsenals have escalated, particularly in the two superpowers. The qualitative superiority of these two states, however, should not overshadow the fact that four other countries

---

56. Paul VI, "World Day of Peace Message 1976," in *Documents*, p. 198.

possess nuclear capacity and a score of states are only steps away from becoming "nuclear nations."

128.   This nuclear escalation has been opposed sporadically and selectively but never effectively. The race has continued in spite of carefully expressed doubts by analysts and other citizens and in the face of forcefully expressed opposition by public rallies. Today the opposition to the arms race is no longer selective or sporadic, it is widespread and sustained. The danger and destructiveness of nuclear weapons are understood and resisted with new urgency and intensity. There is in the public debate today an endorsement of the position submitted by the Holy See at the United Nations in 1976: the arms race is to be condemned as a danger, an act of aggression against the poor, and a folly which does not provide the security it promises.[57]

129.   Papal teaching has consistently addressed the folly and danger of the arms race; but the new perception of it which is now held by the general public is due in large measure to the work of scientists and physicians who have described for citizens the concrete human consequences of a nuclear war.[58]

130.   In a striking demonstration of his personal and pastoral concern for preventing nuclear war, Pope John Paul II commissioned a study by the Pontifical Academy of Sciences which reinforced the findings of other scientific bodies. The Holy Father had the study transmitted by personal representative to the leaders of the United States, the Soviet Union, the United Kingdom, and France, and to the president of the General Assembly of the United Nations. One of its conclusions is especially pertinent to the public debate in the United States:

> Recent talk about winning or even surviving a nuclear war must reflect a failure to appreciate a medical reality: Any nuclear war would inevitably cause death, disease and suffering of pandemonic proportions and without the possibility of effective medical intervention. That reality leads to the same conclusion physicians have reached for life-threatening epidemics throughout history. Prevention is essential for control.[59]

131.   This medical conclusion has a moral corollary. Traditionally, the Church's moral teaching sought first to prevent war and then to

---

57. "Statement of the Holy See to the United Nations" (1976), in *The Church and the Arms Race*; Pax Christi-USA (New York: 1976), pp. 23-24.

58. R. Adams and S. Cullen, *The Final Epidemic: Physicians and Scientists on Nuclear War* (Chicago: 1981).

59. Pontifical Academy of Sciences, "Statement on the Consequences of the Use of Nuclear Weapons," in *Documents*, p. 241.

limit its consequences if it occurred. Today the possibilities for placing political and moral limits on nuclear war are so minimal that the moral task, like the medical, is prevention: as a people, we must refuse to legitimate the idea of nuclear war. Such a refusal will require not only new ideas and new vision, but what the gospel calls conversion of the heart.

132. To say "no" to nuclear war is both a necessary and a complex task. We are moral teachers in a tradition which has always been prepared to relate moral principles to concrete problems. Particularly in this letter we could not be content with simply restating general moral principles or repeating well-known requirements about the ethics of war. We have had to examine, with the assistance of a broad spectrum of advisors of varying persuasions, the nature of existing and proposed weapons systems, the doctrines which govern their use, and the consequences of using them. We have consulted people who engage their lives in protest against the existing nuclear strategy of the United States, and we have consulted others who have held or do hold responsibility for this strategy. It has been a sobering and perplexing experience. In light of the evidence which witnesses presented and in light of our study, reflection, and consultation, we must reject nuclear war. But we feel obliged to relate our judgment to the specific elements which comprise the nuclear problem.

133. Though certain that the dangerous and delicate nuclear relationship the superpowers now maintain should not exist, we understand how it came to exist. In a world of sovereign states, devoid of central authority and possessing the knowledge to produce nuclear weapons, many choices were made, some clearly objectionable, others well-intended with mixed results, which brought the world to its present dangerous situation.

134. We see with increasing clarity the political folly of a system which threatens mutual suicide, the psychological damage this does to ordinary people, especially the young, the economic distortion of priorities—billions readily spent for destructive instruments while pitched battles are waged daily in our legislatures over much smaller amounts for the homeless, the hungry, and the helpless here and abroad. But it is much less clear how we translate a "no" to nuclear war into the personal and public choices which can move us in a new direction, toward a national policy and an international system which more adequately reflect the values and vision of the kingdom of God.

135. These tensions in our assessment of the politics and strategy of the nuclear age reflect the conflicting elements of the nuclear dilemma and the balance of terror which it has produced. We have said earlier in this letter that the fact of war reflects the existence of sin in the world. The nuclear threat and the danger it poses to human life and civilization exemplify in a qualitatively new way the perennial struggle of the political community to contain the use of force, particularly among states.

136.   Precisely because of the destructive nature of nuclear weapons, strategies have been developed which previous generations would have found unintelligible. Today military preparations are undertaken on a vast and sophisticated scale, but the declared purpose is not to use the weapons produced. Threats are made which would be suicidal to implement. The key to security is no longer only military secrets, for in some instances security may best be served by informing one's adversary publicly what weapons one has and what plans exist for their use. The presumption of the nation-state system, that sovereignty implies an ability to protect a nation's territory and population, is precisely the presumption denied by the nuclear capacities of both superpowers. In a sense each is at the mercy of the other's perception of what strategy is "rational," what kind of damage is "unacceptable," how "convincing" one side's threat is to the other.

137.   The political paradox of deterrence has also strained our moral conception. May a nation threaten what it may never do? May it possess what it may never use? Who is involved in the threat each superpower makes: government officials? or military personnel? or the citizenry in whose defense the threat is made?

138.   In brief, the danger of the situation is clear; but how to prevent the use of nuclear weapons, how to assess deterrence, and how to delineate moral responsibility in the nuclear age are less clearly seen or stated. Reflecting the complexity of the nuclear problem, our arguments in this pastoral must be detailed and nuanced; but our "no" to nuclear war must, in the end, be definitive and decisive.

B. Religious Leadership and the Public Debate

139.   Because prevention of nuclear war appears, from several perspectives, to be not only the surest but only way to limit its destructive potential, we see our role as moral teachers precisely in terms of helping to form public opinion with a clear determination to resist resort to nuclear war as an instrument of national policy. If "prevention is the only cure," then there are diverse tasks to be performed in preventing what should never occur. As bishops we see

a specific task defined for us in Pope John Paul II's "World Day of Peace Message 1982":

> Peace cannot be built by the power of rulers alone. Peace can be firmly constructed only if it corresponds to the resolute determination of all people of good will. Rulers must be supported and enlightened by a public opinion that encourages them or, where necessary, expresses disapproval.[60]

140.   The pope's appeal to form public opinion is not an abstract task. Especially in a democracy, public opinion can passively acquiesce in policies and strategies or it can, through a series of measures, indicate the limits beyond which a government should not proceed. The "new moment" which exists in the public debate about nuclear weapons provides a creative opportunity and a moral imperative to examine the relationship between public opinion and public policy. We believe it is necessary, for the sake of prevention, to build a barrier against the concept of nuclear war as a viable strategy for defense. There should be a clear public resistance to the rhetoric of "winnable" nuclear wars, or unrealistic expectations of "surviving" nuclear exchanges, and strategies of "protracted nuclear war." We oppose such rhetoric.

141.   We seek to encourage a public attitude which sets stringent limits on the kind of actions our own government and other governments will take on nuclear policy. We believe religious leaders have a task in concert with public officials, analysts, private organizations, and the media to set the limits beyond which our military policy should not move in word or action. Charting a moral course in a complex public policy debate involves several steps. We will address four questions, offering our reflections on them as an invitation to a public moral dialogue:

1) the use of nuclear weapons;
2) the policy of deterrence in principle and in practice;
3) specific steps to reduce the danger of war;
4) long-term measures of policy and diplomacy.

C. The Use of Nuclear Weapons

142.   Establishing moral guildelines in the nuclear debate means

---

60. John Paul II, "World Day of Peace Message 1982," #6, cited, p. 476.

addressing first the question of the use of nuclear weapons. That question has several dimensions.

143. It is clear that those in the Church who interpret the gospel teaching as forbidding all use of violence would oppose any use of nuclear weapons under any conditions. In a sense the existence of these weapons simply confirms and reinforces one of the initial insights of the non-violent position, namely, that Christians should not use lethal force since the hope of using it selectively and restrictively is so often an illusion. Nuclear weapons seem to prove this point in a way heretofore unknown.

144. For the tradition which acknowledges some legitimate use of force, some important elements of contemporary nuclear strategies move beyond the limits of moral justification. A justifiable use of force must be both discriminatory and proportionate. Certain aspects of both U.S. and Soviet strategies fail both tests as we shall discuss below. The technical literature and the personal testimony of public officials who have been closely associated with U.S. nuclear strategy have both convinced us of the overwhelming probability that major nuclear exchange would have no limits.[61]

145. On the more complicated issue of "limited" nuclear war, we are aware of the extensive literature and discussion which this topic

---

61. The following quotations are from public officials who have served at the highest policy levels in recent administrations of our government: "It is time to recognize that no one has ever succeeded in advancing any persuasive reason to believe that any use of nuclear weapons, even on the smallest scale, could reliably be expected to remain limited." M. Bundy, G. F. Kennan, R. S. McNamara and G. Smith, "Nuclear Weapons and the Atlantic Alliance," *Foreign Affairs* 60 (1982):757.

"From my experience in combat there is no way that [nuclear escalation] . . . can be controlled because of the lack of information, the pressure of time and the deadly results that are taking place on both sides of the battle line." Gen. A. S. Collins, Jr. (former deputy commander in chief of U.S. Army in Europe), "Theatre Nuclear Warfare: The Battlefield," in J. F. Reichart and S. R. Sturn, eds., *American Defense Policy*, 5th ed., (Baltimore: 1982), pp. 359-60.

"None of this potential flexibility changes my view that a full-scale thermonuclear exchange would be an unprecedented disaster for the Soviet Union as well as for the United States. Nor is it at all clear that an initial use of nuclear weapons—however selectively they might be targeted—could be kept from escalating to a full-scale thermonuclear exchange, especially if command-and-control centers were brought under attack. The odds are high, whether weapons were used against tactical or strategic targets, that control would be lost on both sides and the exchange would become unconstrained." Harold Brown, *Department of Defense Annual Report FY 1979* (Washington, D.C.: 1978).

Cf. also: *The Effects of Nuclear War* (Washington, D.C.: 1979, U.S. Government Printing Office).

has generated.[62] As a general statement, it seems to us that public officials would be unable to refute the following conclusion of the study made by the Pontifical Academy of Sciences:

> Even a nuclear attack directed only at military facilities would be devastating to the country as a whole. This is because military facilities are widespread rather than concentrated at only a few points. Thus, many nuclear weapons would be exploded.
>
> Furthermore, the spread of radiation due to the natural winds and atmospheric mixing would kill vast numbers of people and contaminate large areas. The medical facilities of any nation would be inadequate to care for the survivors. An objective examination of the medical situation that would follow a nuclear war leads to but one conclusion: prevention is our only recourse.[63]

Moral Principles and Policy Choices

146. In light of these perspectives we address three questions more explicitly: (1) counter population warfare; (2) initiation of nuclear war; and (3) limited nuclear war.

1. Counter Population Warfare

147. Under no circumstances may nuclear weapons or other instruments of mass slaughter be used for the purpose of destroying population centers or other predominantly civilian targets. Popes have repeatedly condemned "total war" which implies such use. For example, as early as 1954 Pope Pius XII condemned nuclear warfare "when it entirely escapes the control of man," and results in "the pure and simple annihilation of all human life within the radius of action."[64] The condemnation was repeated by the Second Vatican Council:

> Any act of war aimed indiscriminately at the destruction of entire cities or of extensive areas along with their population is a crime against God and man itself. It merits unequivocal and unhesitating condemnation.[65]

---

62. For example, cf.: H. A. Kissinger, *Nuclear Weapons and Foreign Policy* (New York: 1957), *The Necessity for Choice* (New York: 1960); R. Osgood and R. Tucker, *Force, Order and Justice* (Baltimore: 1967); R. Aron, *The Great Debate: Theories of Nuclear Strategy* (New York: 1965); D. Ball, *Can Nuclear War Be Controlled?* Adelphi Paper #161 (London: 1981); M. Howard, "On Fighting a Nuclear War," *International Security* 5 (1981):3-17.

63. "Statement on the Consequences of the Use of Nuclear Weapons," cited, p. 243.

64. Pius XII, "Address to the VIII Congress of the World Medical Association," in *Documents*, p. 131.

65. *Pastoral Constitution*, #80.

148.   Retaliatory action whether nuclear or conventional which would indiscriminately take many wholly innocent lives, lives of people who are in no way responsible for reckless actions of their government, must also be condemned. This condemnation, in our judgment, applies even to the retaliatory use of weapons striking enemy cities after our own have already been struck. No Christian can rightfully carry out orders or policies deliberately aimed at killing non-combatants.[66]

149.   We make this judgment at the beginning of our treatment of nuclear strategy precisely because the defense of the principle of non-combatant immunity is so important for an ethic of war and because the nuclear age has posed such extreme problems for the principle. Later in this letter we shall discuss specific aspects of U.S. policy in light of this principle and in light of recent U.S. policy statements stressing the determination not to target directly or strike directly against civilian populations. Our concern about protecting the moral value of noncombatant immunity, however, requires that we make a clear reassertion of the principle our first word on this matter.

2. The Initiation of Nuclear War

150.   We do not perceive any situation in which the deliberate initiation of nuclear warfare, on however restricted a scale, can be morally justified. Non-nuclear attacks by another state must be resisted by other than nuclear means. Therefore, a serious moral obligation exists to develop non-nuclear defensive strategies as rapidly as possible.

151.   A serious debate is under way on this issue.[67] It is cast in political terms, but it has a significant moral dimension. Some have argued that at the very beginning of a war nuclear weapons might be used, only against military targets, perhaps in limited numbers. Indeed it has long been American and NATO policy that nuclear weapons, especially so-called tactical nuclear weapons, would likely be used if NATO forces in Europe seemed in danger of losing a conflict that until then had been restricted to conventional weapons. Large numbers of tactical nuclear weapons are now deployed in Europe by the NATO forces and about as many by the Soviet Union. Some are substantially smaller than the bomb used on Hiroshima,

---

66. Ibid.

67. M. Bundy, et al., "Nuclear Weapons," cited; K. Kaiser, G. Leber, A. Mertes, F. J. Schulze, "Nuclear Weapons and the Preservation of Peace," *Foreign Affairs* 60 (1982):1157-70; cf. other responses to Bundy article in the same issue of *Foreign Affairs*.

some are larger. Such weapons, if employed in great numbers, would totally devastate the densely populated countries of Western and Central Europe.

152. Whether under conditions of war in Europe, parts of Asia or the Middle East, or the exchange of strategic weapons directly between the United States and the Soviet Union, the difficulties of limiting the use of nuclear weapons are immense. A number of expert witnesses advise us that commanders operating under conditions of battle probably would not be able to exercise strict control; the number of weapons used would rapidly increase, the targets would be expanded beyond the military, and the level of civilian casualties would rise enormously.[68] No one can be certain that this escalation would not occur, even in the face of political efforts to keep such an exchange "limited." The chances of keeping use limited seem remote, and the consequences of escalation to mass destruction would be appalling. Former public officials have testified that it is improbable that any nuclear war could actually be kept limited. Their testimony and the consequences involved in this problem lead us to conclude that the danger of escalation is so great that it would be morally unjustifiable to initiate nuclear war in any form. The danger is rooted not only in the technology of our weapons systems but in the weakness and sinfulness of human communities. We find the moral responsibility of beginning nuclear war not justified by rational political objectives.

153. This judgment affirms that the willingness to initiate nuclear war entails a distinct, weighty moral responsibility; it involves transgressing a fragile barrier—political, psychological, and moral—which has been constructed since 1945. We express repeatedly in this letter our extreme skepticism about the prospects for controlling a nuclear exchange, however limited the first use might be. Precisely because of this skepticism, we judge resort to nuclear weapons to counter a conventional attack to be morally unjustifiable.[69] Consequently we seek to reinforce the barrier against any use of nuclear weapons. Our support of a "no first use" policy must be seen in this light.

154. At the same time we recognize the responsibility the United States has had and continues to have in assisting allied nations in their defense against either a conventional or a nuclear attack. Es-

---

68. Testimony given to the National Conference of Catholic Bishops Committee during preparation of this pastoral letter. The testimony is reflected in the quotes found in note 61.

69. Our conclusions and judgments in this area although based on careful study and reflection of the application of moral principles do not have, of course, the same force as the principles themselves and therefore allow for different opinions, as the Summary makes clear.

pecially in the European theater, the deterrence of a *nuclear* attack may require nuclear weapons for a time, even though their possession and deployment must be subject to rigid restrictions.

155.   The need to defend against a conventional attack in Europe imposes the political and moral burden of developing adequate, alternative modes of defense to present reliance on nuclear weapons. Even with the best coordinated effort—hardly likely in view of contemporary political division on this question—development of an alternative defense position will still take time.

156.   In the interim, deterrence against a conventional attack relies upon two factors: the not inconsiderable conventional forces at the disposal of NATO and the recognition by a potential attacker that the outbreak of large scale conventional war could escalate to the nuclear level through accident or miscalculation by either side. We are aware that NATO's refusal to adopt a "no first use" pledge is to some extent linked to the deterrent effect of this inherent ambiguity. Nonetheless, in light of the probable effects of initiating nuclear war, we urge NATO to move rapidly toward the adoption of a "no first use" policy, but doing so in tandem with development of an adequate alternative defense posture.

3. Limited Nuclear War

157.   It would be possible to agree with our first two conclusions and still not be sure about retaliatory use of nuclear weapons in what is called a "limited exchange." The issue at stake is the *real* as opposed to the *theoretical* possibility of a "limited nuclear exchange."

158.   We recognize that the policy debate on this question is inconclusive and that all participants are left with hypothetical projections about probable reactions in a nuclear exchange. While not trying to adjudicate the technical debate, we are aware of it and wish to raise a series of questions which challenge the actual meaning of "limited" in this discussion.

—Would leaders have sufficient information to know what is happening in a nuclear exchange?

—Would they be able under the conditions of stress, time pressures, and fragmentary information to make the extraordinarily precise decision needed to keep the exchange limited if this were technically possible?

—Would military commanders be able, in the midst of the destruction and confusion of a nuclear exchange, to maintain a policy of "discriminate targeting"? Can this be done in modern warfare, waged across great distances by aircraft and missiles?

—Given the accidents we know about in peacetime conditions, what assurances are there that computer errors could be avoided in the midst of a nuclear exchange?

—Would not the casualties, even in a war defined as limited by strategists, still run in the millions?

—How "limited" would be the long-term effects of radiation, famine, social fragmentation, and economic dislocation?

159. Unless these questions can be answered satisfactorily, we will continue to be highly skeptical about the real meaning of "limited." One of the criteria of the just-war tradition is a reasonable hope of success in bringing about justice and peace. We must ask whether such a reasonable hope can exist once nuclear weapons have been exchanged. The burden of proof remains on those who assert that meaningful limitation is possible.

160. A nuclear response to either conventional or nuclear attack can cause destruction which goes far beyond "legitimate defense." Such use of nuclear weapons would not be justified.

161. In the face of this frightening and highly speculative debate on a matter involving millions of human lives, we believe the most effective contribution of moral judgment is to introduce perspectives by which we can assess the empirical debate. Moral perspective should be sensitive not only to the quantitative dimensions of a question but to its psychological, human, and religious characteristics as well. The issue of limited war is not simply the size of weapons contemplated or the strategies projected. The debate should include the psychological and political significance of crossing the boundary from the conventional to the nuclear arena in any form. To cross this divide is to enter a world where we have no experience of control, much testimony against its possibility, and therefore no moral justification for submitting the human community to this risk.[70] We therefore express our view that the first imperative is to prevent any use of nuclear weapons and our hope that leaders will resist the notion that nuclear conflict can be limited, contained, or won in any traditional sense.

---

70. Undoubtedly aware of the long and detailed technical debate on limited war, Pope John Paul II highlighted the unacceptable moral risk of crossing the threshold to nuclear war in his "Angelus Message" of December 13, 1981: "I have, in fact, the deep conviction that, in the light of a nuclear war's effects, which can be scientifically foreseen as certain, the only choice that is morally and humanly valid is represented by the reduction of nuclear armaments, while waiting for their future complete elimination, carried out simultaneously by all the parties, by means of explicit agreements and with the commitment of accepting effective controls." In *Documents*, p. 240.

D. Deterrence in Principle and Practice

162. The moral challenge posed by nuclear weapons is not exhausted by an analysis of their possible uses. Much of the political and moral debate of the nuclear age has concerned the strategy of deterrence. Deterrence is at the heart of the U.S.-Soviet relationship, currently the most dangerous dimension of the nuclear arms race.

1. The Concept and Development of Deterrence Policy

163. The concept of deterrence existed in military strategy long before the nuclear age, but it has taken on a new meaning and significance since 1945. Essentially, deterrence means "dissuasion of a potential adversary from initiating an attack or conflict, often by the threat of unacceptable retaliatory damage."[71] In the nuclear age, deterrence has become the centerpiece of both U.S. and Soviet policy. Both superpowers have for many years now been able to promise a retaliatory response which can inflict "unacceptable damage." A situation of stable deterrence depends on the ability of each side to deploy its retaliatory forces in ways that are not vulnerable to an attack (i.e., protected against a "first strike"); preserving stability requires a willingness by both sides to refrain from deploying weapons which appear to have a first strike capability.

164. This general definition of deterrence does not explain either the elements of a deterrence strategy or the evolution of deterrence policy since 1945. A detailed description of either of these subjects would require an extensive essay, using materials which can be found in abundance in the technical literature on the subject of deterrence.[72] Particularly significant is the relationship between "declaratory policy" (the public explanation of our strategic intentions and capabilities) and "action policy" (the actual planning and targeting policies to be followed in a nuclear attack).

---

71. W. H. Kincade and J. D. Porro, *Negotiating Security: An Arms Control Reader* (Washington, D.C.: 1979).

72. Several surveys are available, for example cf.: J. H. Kahin, *Security in the Nuclear Age: Developing U.S. Strategic Policy* (Washington, D.C.: 1975); M. Mandelbaum, *The Nuclear Question: The United States and Nuclear Weapons 1946-1976* (Cambridge, England: 1979); B. Brodie, "Development of Nuclear Strategy," *International Security* 2 (1978):65-83.

165.   The evolution of deterrence strategy has passed through several stages of declaratory policy. Using the U.S. case as an example, there is a significant difference between "massive retaliation" and "flexible response," and between "mutual assured destruction" and "countervailing strategy." It is also possible to distinguish between "counterforce" and "countervalue" targeting policies; and to contrast a posture of "minimum deterrence" with "extended deterrence." These terms are well known in the technical debate on nuclear policy; they are less well known and sometimes loosely used in the wider public debate. It is important to recognize that there has been substantial continuity in U.S. action policy in spite of real changes in declaratory policy.[73]

166.   The recognition of these different elements in the deterrent and the evolution of policy means that moral assessment of deterrence requires a series of distinct judgments. They include: an analysis of the *factual character* of the deterrent (e.g., what is involved in targeting doctrine); analysis of the *historical development* of the policy (e.g., whether changes have occurred which are significant for moral analysis of the policy): the relationship of deterrence policy and other aspects of *U.S.-Soviet affairs*; and determination of the key *moral questions* involved in deterrence policy.

2. The Moral Assessment of Deterrence

167.   The distinctively new dimensions of nuclear deterrence were recognized by policymakers and strategists only after much reflection. Similarly, the moral challenge posed by nuclear deterrence was grasped only after careful deliberation. The moral and political paradox posed by deterrence was concisely stated by Vatican II:

> Undoubtedly, armaments are not amassed merely for use in wartime. Since the defensive strength of any nation is thought to depend on its capacity for immediate retaliation, the stockpiling of arms which grows from year to year serves, in a way hitherto unthought of, as a deterrent to potential attackers. Many people look upon this as the most effective way known at the present time for maintaining some sort of peace among nations. Whatever one may think of this form of deterrent, people are convinced that the arms race, which quite a few countries have entered, is no infallible way of maintaining real peace and that the resulting so-called balance of power is no sure genuine path to achieving it. Rather than eliminate the causes of war, the arms race serves only to aggravate the position. As

---

73. The relationship of these two levels of policy is the burden of an article by D. Ball, "U.S. Strategic Forces: How Would They Be Used?" *International Security* 7 (1982/83):31-60

long as extravagent sums of money are poured into the development of
new weapons, it is impossible to devote adequate aid in tackling the misery
which prevails at the present day in the world. Instead of eradicating
international conflict once and for all, the contagion is spreading to other
parts of the world. New approaches, based on reformed attitudes, will have
to be chosen in order to remove this stumbling block, to free the earth
from its pressing anxieties, and give back to the world a genuine peace.[74]

168.   Without making a specific moral judgment on deterrence,
the council clearly designated the elements of the arms race: the
tension between "peace of a sort" preserved by deterrence and "genuine peace" required for a stable international life; the contradiction
between what is spent for destructive capacity and what is needed
for constructive development.

169.   In the post-conciliar assessment of war and peace, and specifically of deterrence, different parties to the political-moral debate
within the Church and in civil society have focused on one aspect
or another of the problem. For some, the fact that nuclear weapons
have not been used since 1945 means that deterrence has worked,
and this fact satisfies the demands of both the political and the moral
order. Others contest this assessment by highlighting the risk of failure
involved in continued reliance on deterrence and pointing out how
politically and morally catastrophic even a single failure would be.
Still others note that the absence of nuclear war is not necessarily
proof that the policy of deterrence has prevented it. Indeed, some
would find in the policy of deterrence the driving force in the superpower arms race. Still other observers, many of them Catholic
moralists, have stressed that deterrence may not morally include the
intention of deliberately attacking civilian populations or non-combatants.

170.   The statements of the NCCB/USCC over the past several
years have both reflected and contributed to the wider moral debate
on deterrence. In the NCCB pastoral letter, *To Live In Christ Jesus*
(1976), we focused on the moral limits of declaratory policy while
calling for stronger measures of arms control.[75] In 1979 John Cardinal
Krol, speaking for the USCC in support of SALT II ratification,
brought into focus the other element of the deterrence problem: the
actual use of nuclear weapons may have been prevented (a moral
good), but the risk of failure and the physical harm and moral evil

---

74. *Pastoral Constitution*, #81.

75. United States Catholic Conference, *To Live in Christ Jesus* (Washington, D.C.: 1976),
p. 34.

resulting from possible nuclear war remained. "This explains," Cardinal Krol stated, "the Catholic dissatisfaction with nuclear deterrence and the urgency of the Catholic demand that the nuclear arms race be reversed. It is of the utmost importance that negotiations proceed to meaningful and continuing reductions in nuclear stockpiles, and eventually to the phasing out altogether of nuclear deterrence and the threat of mutual-assured destruction."[76]

171. These two texts, along with the conciliar statement, have influenced much of Catholic opinion expressed recently on the nuclear question.

172. In June 1982, Pope John Paul II provided new impetus and insight to the moral analysis with his statement to the United Nations Second Special Session on Disarmament. The pope first situated the problem of deterrence within the context of world politics. No power, he observes, will admit to wishing to start a war, but each distrusts others and considers it necessary to mount a strong defense against attack. He then discusses the notion of deterrence:

> Many even think that such preparations constitute the way—even the only way—to safeguard peace in some fashion or at least to impede to the utmost in an efficacious way the outbreak of wars, especially major conflicts which might lead to the ultimate holocaust of humanity and the destruction of the civilization that man has constructed so laboriously over the centuries.
>
> In this approach one can see the "philosophy of peace" which was proclaimed in the ancient Roman principle: *Si vis pacem, para bellum.* Put in modern terms, this "philosophy" has the label of "deterrence" and one can find it in various guises of the search for a "balance of forces" which sometimes has been called, and not without reason, the "balance of terror."[77]

173. Having offered this analysis of the general concept of deterrence, the Holy Father introduces his considerations on disarmament, especially, but not only, nuclear disarmament. Pope John Paul II makes this statement about the morality of deterrence:

> In current conditions "deterrence" based on balance, certainly not as an end in itself but as a step on the way toward a progressive disarmament, may still be judged morally acceptable. Nonetheless in order to ensure peace, it is indispensable not to be satisfied with this minimum which is always susceptible to the real danger of explosion.[78]

---

76. John Cardinal Krol, "Testimony on Salt II," *Origins* (1979):197.

77. John Paul II, "Message U.N. Special Session 1982," #3.

78. Ibid., #8.

174. In Pope John Paul II's assessment we perceive two dimensions of the contemporary dilemma of deterrence. One dimension is the danger of nuclear war, with its human and moral costs. The possession of nuclear weapons, the continuing quantitative growth of the arms race, and the danger of nuclear proliferation all point to the grave danger of basing "peace of a sort" on deterrence. The other dimension is the independence and freedom of nations and entire peoples, including the need to protect smaller nations from threats to their independence and integrity. Deterrence reflects the radical distrust which marks international politics, a condition identified as a major problem by Pope John XIII in *Peace on Earth* and reaffirmed by Pope Paul VI and Pope John Paul II. Thus a balance of forces, preventing either side from achieving superiority, can be seen as a means of safeguarding both dimensions.

175. The moral duty today is to prevent nuclear war from ever occurring *and* to protect and preserve those key values of justice, freedom and independence which are necessary for personal dignity and national integrity. In reference to these issues, Pope John Paul II judges that deterrence may still be judged morally acceptable, "certainly not as an end in itself but as a step on the way toward a progressive disarmament."

176. On more than one occasion the Holy Father has demonstrated his awareness of the fragility and complexity of the deterrence relationship among nations. Speaking to UNESCO in June 1980, he said:

> Up to the present, we are told that nuclear arms are a force of dissuasion which have prevented the eruption of a major war. And that is probably true. Still, we must ask if it will always be this way.[79]

In a more recent and more specific assessment Pope John Paul II told an international meeting of scientists on August 23, 1982:

> You can more easily ascertain that the logic of nuclear deterrence cannot be considered a final goal or an appropriate and secure means for safeguarding international peace.[80]

177. Relating Pope John Paul's general statements to the specific policies of the U.S. deterrent requires both judgments of fact and an application of moral principles. In preparing this letter we have tried,

---

79. John Paul II, "Address to UNESCO, 1980," #21.

80. John Paul II, "Letter to International Seminar on the World implications of a Nuclear Conflict," August 23, 1982, text in *NC News Documentary*, August 24, 1982.

through a number of sources, to determine as precisely as possible the factual character of U.S. deterrence strategy. Two questions have particularly concerned us: 1) the targeting doctrine and strategic plans for the use of the deterrent, particularly their impact on civilian casualties; and 2) the relationship of deterrence strategy and nuclear war-fighting capability to the likelihood that war will in fact be prevented.

Moral Principles and Policy Choices

178.   Targeting doctrine raises significant moral questions because it is a significant determinant of what would occur if nuclear weapons were ever to be used. Although we acknowledge the need for deterrent, not all forms of deterrence are morally acceptable. There are moral limits to deterrence policy as well as to policy regarding use. Specifically, it is not morally acceptable to intend to kill the innocent as part of a strategy of deterring nuclear war. The question of whether U.S. policy involves an intention to strike civilian centers (directly targeting civilian populations) has been one of our factual concerns. *179.*   This complex question has always produced a variety of responses, official and unofficial in character. The NCCB Committee has received a series of statements of clarification of policy from U.S. government officials.[81] Essentially these statements declare that it is not U.S. strategic policy to target the Soviet civilian population as such or to use nuclear weapons deliberately for the purpose of destroying population centers. These statements respond, in principle at least, to one moral criterion for assessing deterrence policy: the immunity of non-combatants from direct attack either by conventional or nuclear weapons.

---

81. Particularly helpful was the letter of January 15, 1983, of Mr. William Clark, national security adviser, to Cardinal Bernardin. Mr. Clark stated: "For moral, political and military reasons, the United States does not target the Soviet civilian population as such. There is no deliberately opaque meaning conveyed in the last two words. We do not threaten the existence of Soviet civilization by threatening Soviet cities. Rather, we hold at risk the war-making capability of the Soviet Union—its armed forces, and the industrial capacity to sustain war. It would be irresponsible for us to issue policy statements which might suggest to the Soviets that it would be to their advantage to establish privileged sanctuaries within heavily populated areas, thus inducing them to locate much of their war-fighting capability within those urban sanctuaries." A reaffirmation of the administration's policy is also found in Secretary Weinberger's *Annual Report to the Congress* (Caspar Weinberger, *Annual Report to the Congress*, February 1, 1983, p. 55): "The Reagan Administration's policy is that under no circumstances may such weapons be used deliberately for the purpose of destroying populations." Also the letter of Mr. Weinberger to Bishop O'Connor of February 9, 1983, has a similar statement.

180. These statements do not address or resolve another very troublesome moral problem, namely, that an attack on military targets or militarily significant industrial targets could involve "indirect" (i.e., unintended) but massive civilian casualties. We are advised, for example, that the United States strategic nuclear targeting plan (SIOP—Single Integrated Operational Plan) has identified 60 "military" targets within the city of Moscow alone, and that 40,000 "military" targets for nuclear weapons have been identified in the whole of the Soviet Union.[82] It is important to recognize that Soviet policy is subject to the same moral judgment; attacks on several "industrial targets" or politically significant targets in the United States could produce massive civilian casualties. The number of civilians who would necessarily be killed by such strikes is horrendous.[83] This problem is unavoidable because of the way modern military facilities and production centers are so thoroughly interspersed with civilian living and working areas. It is aggravated if one side deliberately positions military targets in the midst of a civilian population. In our consultations, administration officials readily admitted that, while they hoped any nuclear exchange could be kept limited, they were prepared to retaliate in a massive way if necessary. They also agreed that once any substantial numbers of weapons were used, the civilian casualty levels would quickly become truly catastrophic, and that even with attacks limited to "military" targets, the number of deaths in a substantial exchange would be almost indistinguishable from what might occur if civilian centers had been deliberately and directly struck. These possibilities pose a different moral question and are to be judged by a different moral criterion: the principle of proportionality.

181. While any judgment of proportionality is always open to differing evaluations, there are actions which can be decisively judged to be disproportionate. A narrow adherence exclusively to the principle of noncombatant immunity as a criterion for policy is an inadequate moral posture for it ignores some evil and unacceptable consequences. Hence, we cannot be satisfied that the assertion of an intention not to strike civilians directly, or even the most honest effort to implement that intention, by itself constitutes a "moral policy" for the use of nuclear weapons.

---

82. S. Zuckerman, *Nuclear Illusion and Reality* (New York: 1982); D. Ball, cited, p. 36; T. Powers, "Choosing a Strategy for World War III," *The Atlantic Monthly*, November 1982, pp. 82-110.

83. Cf. the comments in Pontifical Academy of Sciences "Statement on the Consequences of the Use of Nuclear Weapons," cited.

182. The location of industrial or militarily significant economic targets within heavily populated areas or in those areas affected by radioactive fallout could well involve such massive civilian casualties that, in our judgment, such a strike would be deemed morally disproportionate, even though not intentionally indiscriminate.

183. The problem is not simply one of producing highly accurate weapons that might mirimize civilian casualties in any single explosion, but one of increasing the likelihood of escalation at a level where many, even "discriminating," weapons would cumulatively kill very large numbers of civilians. Those civilian deaths would occur both immediately and from the long-term effects of social and economic devastation.

184. A second issue of concern to us is the relationship of deterrence doctrine to war-fighting strategies. We are aware of the argument that war-fighting capabilities enhance the credibility of the deterrent, particularly the strategy of extended deterrence. But the development of such capabilities raises other strategic and moral questions. The relationship of war-fighting capabilities and targeting doctrine exemplifies the difficult choices in this area of policy. Targeting civilian populations would violate the principle of discrimination—one of the central moral principles of a Christian ethic of war. But "counterforce targeting," while preferable from the perspective of protecting civilians, is often joined with a declaratory policy which conveys the notion that nuclear war is subject to precise rational and moral limits. We have already expressed our severe doubts about such a concept. Furthermore, a purely counterforce strategy may seem to threaten the viability of other nations' retaliatory forces, making deterrence unstable in a crisis and war more likely.

185. While we welcome any effort to protect civilian populations, we do not want to legitimize or encourage moves which extend deterrence beyond the specific objective of preventing the use of nuclear weapons or other actions which could lead directly to a nuclear exchange.

186. These considerations of concrete elements of nuclear deterrence policy, made in light of John Paul II's evaluation, but applying it through our own prudential judgments, lead us to a strictly conditioned moral acceptance of nuclear deterrence. We cannot consider it adequate as a long-term basis for peace.

187. This strictly conditioned judgment yields *criteria* for morally assessing the elements of deterrence strategy. Clearly, these criteria demonstrate that we cannot approve of every weapons system, strategic doctrine, or policy initiative advanced in the name of strengthening deterrence. On the contrary, these criteria require continual public scrutiny of what our government proposes to do with the deterrent.

188.   *On the basis of these criteria we wish now to make some specific evaluations*:

1) If nuclear deterrence exists only to prevent the *use* of nuclear weapons by others, then proposals to go beyond this to planning for prolonged periods of repeated nuclear strikes and counter-strikes, or "prevailing" in nuclear war, are not acceptable. They encourage notions that nuclear war can be engaged in with tolerable human and moral consequences. Rather, we must continually say "no" to the idea of nuclear war.

2) If nuclear deterrence is our goal, "sufficiency" to deter is an adequate strategy; the quest for nuclear superiority must be rejected.

3) Nuclear deterrence should be used as a step on the way toward progressive disarmanent. Each proposed addition to our strategic system or change in strategic doctrine must be assessed precisely in light of whether it will render steps toward "progressive disarmament" more or less likely.

189.   Moreover, these criteria provide us with the means to make some judgments and recommendations about the present direction of U.S. strategic policy. Progress toward a world freed of dependence on nuclear deterrence must be carefully carried out. But it must not be delayed. There is an urgent moral and political responsibility to use the "peace of a sort" we have as a framework to move toward authentic peace through nuclear arms control, reductions, and disarmament. Of primary importance in this process is the need to prevent the development and deployment of destabilizing weapons systems on either side; a second requirement is to insure that the more sophisticated command and control systems do not become mere hair triggers for automatic launch on warning; a third is the need to prevent the proliferation of nuclear weapons in the international system.

190.   In light of these general judgments *we oppose* some specific proposals in respect to our present deterrence posture:

1) The addition of weapons which are likely to be vulnerable to attack, yet also possess a "prompt hard-target kill" capability that threatens to make the other side's retaliatory forces vulnerable. Such weapons may seem to be useful primarily in a first strike;[84] we resist

---

84. Several experts in strategic theory would place both the MX missile and Pershing II missiles in this category.

such weapons for this reason and we oppose Soviet deployment of such weapons which generate fear of a first strike against U.S. forces.

2) The willingness to foster strategic planning which seeks a nuclear war-fighting capability that goes beyond the limited function of deterrence outlined in this letter.

3) Proposals which have the effect of lowering the nuclear threshold and blurring the difference between nuclear and conventional weapons.

191.   In support of the concept of "sufficiency" as an adequate deterrent, and in light of the present size and composition of both the U.S. and Soviet strategic arsenals, *we recommend*:

1) Support for immediate, bilateral, verifiable agreements to halt the testing, production, and deployment of new nuclear weapons systems.[85]

2) Support for negotiated bilateral deep cuts in the arsenals of both superpowers, particularly those weapons systems which have destabilizing characteristics; U.S. proposals like those for START (Strategic Arms Reduction Talks) and INF (Intermediate-range Nuclear Forces) negotiations in Geneva are said to be designed to achieve deep cuts;[86] our hope is that they will be pursued in a manner which will realize these goals.

3) Support for early and successful conclusion of negotiations of a comprehensive test ban treaty.

4) Removal by all parties of short-range nuclear weapons which multiply dangers disproportionate to their deterrent value.

5) Removal by all parties of nuclear weapons from areas where they are likely to be overrun in the early stages of war, thus forcing rapid and uncontrollable decisions on their use.

6) Strengthening of command and control over nuclear weapons to prevent inadvertent and unauthorized use.

192.   These judgments are meant to exemplify how a lack of unequivocal condemnation of deterrence is meant only to be an attempt to acknowledge the role attributed to deterrence, but not to support its extension beyond the limited purpose discussed above. Some have

---

85. In each of the successive drafts of this letter we have tried to state a central moral imperative: that the arms race should be stopped and disarmament begun. The implementation of this imperative is open to a wide variety of approaches. Hence we have chosen our own language in this paragraph, not wanting either to be identified with one specific political initiative or to have our words used against specific political measures.

86. Cf. President Reagan's "Speech to the National Press Club" (November 18, 1981) and "Address at Eureka College" (May 9, 1982), Department of State, *Current Policy* #346 and #387.

urged us to condemn all aspects of nuclear deterrence. This urging has been based on a variety of reasons, but has emphasized particularly the high and terrible risks that either deliberate use or accidental detonation of nuclear weapons could quickly escalate to something utterly disproportionate to any acceptable moral purpose. That determination requires highly technical judgments about hypothetical events. Although reasons exist which move some to condemn reliance on nuclear weapons for deterrence, we have not reached this conclusion for the reasons outlined in this letter.

193.   Nevertheless, there must be no misunderstanding of our profound skepticism about the moral acceptability of any use of nuclear weapons. It is obvious that the use of any weapons which violate the principle of discrimination merits unequivocal condemnation. We are told that some weapons are designed for purely "counterforce" use against military forces and targets. The moral issue, however, is not resolved by the design of weapons or the planned intention for use; there are also consequences which must be assessed. It would be a perverted political policy or moral casuistry which tried to justify using a weapon which "indirectly" or "unintentionally" killed a million innocent people because they happened to live near a "militarily significant target."

194.   Even the "indirect effects" of initiating nuclear war are sufficient to make it an unjustifiable moral risk in any form. It is not sufficient, for example, to contend that "our" side has plans for "limited" or "discriminate" use. Modern warfare is not readily contained by good intentions or technological designs. The psychological climate of the world is such that mention of the term "nuclear" generates uneasiness. Many contend that the use of one tactical nuclear weapon could produce panic, with completely unpredictable consequences. It is precisely this mix of political, psychological, and technological uncertainty which has moved us in this letter to reinforce with moral prohibitions and prescriptions the prevailing political barrier against resort to nuclear weapons. Our support for enhanced command and control facilities, for major reductions in strategic and tactical nuclear forces, and for a "no first use" policy (as set forth in this letter) is meant to be seen as a complement to our desire to draw a moral line against nuclear war.

195.   Any claim by any government that it is pursuing a morally acceptable policy of deterrence must be scrutinized with the greatest care. We are prepared and eager to participate in our country in the ongoing public debate on moral grounds.

196. The need to rethink the deterrence policy of our nation, to make the revisions necessary to reduce the possibility of nuclear war, and to move toward a more stable system of national and international security will demand a substantial intellectual, political, and moral effort. It also will require, we believe, the willingness to open ourselves to the providential care, power and word of God, which call us to recognize our common humanity and the bonds of mutual responsibility which exist in the international community in spite of political differences and nuclear arsenals.

197. Indeed, we do acknowledge that there are many strong voices within our own episcopal ranks and within the wider Catholic community in the United States which challenge the strategy of deterrence as an adequate response to the arms race today. They highlight the historical evidence that deterrence has not, in fact, set in motion substantial processes of disarmament.

198. Moreover, these voices rightly raise the concern that even the conditional acceptance of nuclear deterrence as laid out in a letter such as this might be inappropriately used by some to reinforce the policy of arms buildup. In its stead, they call us to raise a prophetic challenge to the community of faith—a challenge which goes beyond nuclear deterrence, toward more resolute steps to actual bilateral disarmament and peacemaking. We recognize the intellectual ground on which the argument is built and the religious sensibility which gives it its strong force.

199. The dangers of the nuclear age and the enormous difficulties we face in moving toward a more adequate system of global security, stability and justice require steps beyond our present conceptions of security and defense policy. In the following section we propose a series of steps aimed at a more adequate policy for preserving peace in a nuclear world.

III. The Promotion of Peace: Proposals and Policies

200.   In a world which is not yet the fulfillment of God's kingdom, a world where both personal actions and social forces manifest the continuing influence of sin and disorder among us, consistent attention must be paid to preventing and limiting the violence of war. But this task, addressed extensively in the previous section of this letter, does not exhaust Catholic teaching on war and peace. A complementary theme, reflected in the Scriptures and the theology of the Church and significantly developed by papal teaching in this century, is the building of peace as the way to prevent war. This traditional theme was vividly reasserted by Pope John Paul in his homily at Coventry Cathedral:

> Peace is not just the absence of war. It involves mutual respect and confidence between peoples and nations. It involves collaboration and binding agreements. Like a cathedral, peace must be constructed patiently and with unshakable faith.[87]

201.   This positive conception of peacemaking profoundly influences many people in our time. At the beginning of this letter we affirmed the need for a more fully developed theology of peace. The basis of such a theology is found in the papal teaching of this century. In this section of our pastoral we wish to illustrate how the positive vision of peace contained in Catholic teaching provides direction for policy and personal choices.

A. Specific Steps to Reduce the Danger of War

202.   The dangers of modern war are specific and visible; our

---

87. John Paul II, "Homily at Bagington Airport," Coventry, #2, *Origins* 12 (1982):55.

teaching must be equally specific about the needs of peace. Effective arms control leading to mutual disarmament, ratification of pending treaties,[88] development of nonviolent alternatives, are but some of the recommendations we would place before the Catholic community and all men and women of good will. These should be part of a foreign policy which recognizes and respects the claims of citizens of every nation to the same inalienable rights we treasure, and seeks to ensure an international security based on the awareness that the creator has provided this world and all its resources for the sustenance and benefit of the entire human family. The truth that the globe is inhabited by a single family in which all have the same basic needs and all have a right to the goods of the earth is a fundamental principle of Catholic teaching which we believe to be of increasing importance today. In an interdependent world all need to affirm their common nature and destiny; such a perspective should inform our policy vision and negotiating posture in pursuit of peace today.

1. Accelerated Work for Arms Control, Reduction, and Disarmament

203. Despite serious efforts, starting with the Baruch plans and continuing through SALT I and SALT II, the results have been far too limited and partial to be commensurate with the risks of nuclear war. Yet efforts for negotiated control and reduction of arms must continue. In his 1982 address to the United Nations, Pope John Paul II left no doubt about the importance of these efforts:

> Today once again before you all I reaffirm my confidence in the power of true negotiations to arrive at just and equitable solutions.[89]

204. In this same spirit, we urge negotiations to halt the testing, production, and deployment of new nuclear weapons systems. Not only should steps be taken to end development and deployment, but the numbers of existing weapons must be reduced in a manner which lessens the danger of war.

205. Arms control and disarmament must be a process of verifiable agreements especially between two superpowers. While we do not advocate a policy of unilateral disarmament, we believe the urgent

---

88. The two treaties are the Threshold Test Ban Treaty signed July 3, 1974, and the Treaty on Nuclear Explosions for Peaceful Purposes (P.N.E.) signed May 28, 1976.

89. John Paul II, "Message to U.N. Special Session 1982," #8.

need for control of the arms race requires a willingness for each side to take some first steps. The United States has already taken a number of important independent initiatives to reduce some of the gravest dangers and to encourage a constructive Soviet response; additional initiatives are encouraged. By independent initiatives we mean carefully chosen limited steps which the United States could take for a defined period of time, seeking to elicit a comparable step from the Soviet Union. If an appropriate response is not forthcoming, the United States would no longer be bound by steps taken. Our country has previously taken calculated risks in favor of freedom and of human values; these have included independent steps taken to reduce some of the gravest dangers of nuclear war.[90] Certain risks are required today to help free the world from bondage to nuclear deterrence and the risk of nuclear war. Both sides, for example, have an interest in avoiding deployment of destabilizing weapons systems.

206.   There is some history of successful independent initiatives which have beneficially influenced the arms race without a formal public agreement. In 1963 President Kennedy announced that the United States would unilaterally forgo further nuclear testing; the next month Soviet Premier Nikita Khrushchev proposed a limited test ban which eventually became the basis of the U.S.-Soviet partial test ban treaty. Subsequently, both superpowers removed about 10,000 troops from Central Europe and each announced a cut in production of nuclear material for weapons.

207.   a) Negotiation on arms control agreements in isolation, without persistent and parallel efforts to reduce the political tensions which motivate the buildup of armaments, will not suffice. The United States should therefore have a continuing policy of maximum political engagement with governments of potential adversaries, providing for repeated, systematic discussion and negotiation of areas of friction. This policy should be carried out by a system of periodic, carefully prepared meetings at several levels of government, including summit meetings at regular intervals. Such channels of discussion are too important to be regarded by either of the major powers as a concession or an event made dependent on daily shifts in international developments.

208.   b) The Nuclear Non-Proliferation Treaty of 1968 (NPT) acknowledged that the spread of nuclear weapons to hitherto non-nuclear states (horizontal proliferation) could hardly be prevented in the long run in the absence of serious efforts by the nuclear states to control

---

90. Mr. Weinberger's letter to Bishop O'Connor specifies actions taken on command and control facilities designed to reduce the chance of unauthorized firing of nuclear weapons.

and reduce their own nuclear arsenals (vertical proliferation). Article VI of the NPT pledged the superpowers to serious efforts to control and to reduce their own nuclear arsenals; unfortunately, this promise has not been kept. Moreoever, the multinational controls envisaged in the treaty seem to have been gradually relaxed by the states exporting fissionable materials for the production of energy. If these tendencies are not constrained, the treaty may eventually lose its symbolic and practical effectiveness. For this reason the United States should, in concert with other nuclear exporting states, seriously reexamine its policies and programs and make clear its determination to uphold the spirit as well as the letter of the treaty.

2. Continued Insistence on Efforts to Minimize the Risk of Any War

209. While it is right and proper that priority be given to reducing and ultimately eliminating the likelihood of nuclear war, this does not of itself remove the threat of other forms of warfare. Indeed, negotiated reduction in nuclear weapons available to the superpowers could conceivably increase the danger of non-nuclear wars.

210. a) Because of this we strongly support negotiations aimed at reducing and limiting conventional forces and at building confidence between possible adversaries, especially in regions of potential military confrontations. We urge that prohibitions outlawing the production and use of chemical and biological weapons be reaffirmed and observed. Arms control negotiations must take account of the possibility that conventional conflict could trigger the nuclear confrontation the world must avoid.

211. b) Unfortunately, as is the case with nuclear proliferation, we are witnessing a relaxation of restraints in the international commerce in conventional arms. Sales of increasingly sophisticated military aircraft, missiles, tanks, anti-tank weapons, anti-personnel bombs, and other systems by the major supplying countries (especially the Soviet Union, the United States, France, and Great Britain) have reached unprecedented levels.

212. Pope John Paul II took specific note of the problem in his U.N. address:

The production and sale of conventional weapons throughout the world is a truly alarming and evidently growing phenomenon . . . . Moreover the

66

traffic in these weapons seems to be developing at an increasing rate and seems to be directed most of all toward developing countries.[91]

213. It is a tragic fact that U.S. arms sales policies in the last decade have contributed significantly to the trend the Holy Father deplores. We call for a reversal of this course. The United States should renew earlier efforts to develop multilateral controls on arms exports, and should in this case also be willing to take carefully chosen independent initiatives to restrain the arms trade. Such steps would be particularly appropriate where the receiving government faces charges of gross and systematic human rights violations.[92]

214. c) Nations must accept a limited view of those interests justifying military force. True self-defense may include the protection of weaker states, but does not include seizing the possessions of others, or the domination of other states or peoples. We should remember the caution of Pope John Paul II: "In alleging the threat of a potential enemy, is it really not rather the intention to keep for itself a means of threat, in order to get the upper hand with the aid of one's own arsenal of destruction?"[93] Central to a moral theory of force is the principle that it must be a last resort taken only when *all* other means of redress have been exhausted. Equally important in the age of modern warfare is the recognition that the justifiable reasons for using force have been restricted to instances of self-defense or defense of others under attack.

3. The Relationship of Nuclear and Conventional Defenses

215. The strong position we have taken against the use of nuclear weapons, and particularly the stand against the initiation of nuclear war in any form, calls for further clarification of our view of the requirements for conventional defense.

216. Nuclear threats have often come to take the place of efforts to deter or defend against non-nuclear attack with weapons that are themselves non-nuclear, particularly in the NATO-Warsaw Pact confrontation. Many analysts conclude that, in the absence of nuclear

---

91. Ibid. Cf. United States Catholic Conference, *At Issue #2: Arms Export Policies—Ethical Choices* (Washington, D.C.: 1978) for suggestions about controlling the conventional arms trade.

92. The International Security Act of 1976 provides for such human rights review.

93. John Paul II, "Address to the United Nations General Assembly," *Origins* 9 (1979):268.

deterrent threats, more troops and conventional (non-nuclear) weapons would be required to protect our allies. Rejection of some forms of nuclear deterrence could therefore conceivably require a willingness to pay higher costs to develop conventional forces. Leaders and peoples of other nations might also have to accept higher costs for their own defense, particularly in Western Europe, if the threat to use nuclear weapons first were withdrawn. We cannot judge the strength of these arguments in particular cases. It may well be that some strengthening of conventional defense would be a proportionate price to pay, if this will reduce the possibility of a nuclear war. We acknowledge this reluctantly, aware as we are of the vast amount of scarce resources expended annually on instruments of defense in a world filled with other urgent, unmet human needs.

217. It is not for us to settle the technical debate about policy and budgets. From the perspective of a developing theology of peace, however, we feel obliged to contribute a moral dimension to the discussion. We hope that a significant reduction in numbers of conventional arms and weaponry would go hand in hand with diminishing reliance on nuclear deterrence. The history of recent wars (even so-called "minor" or "limited" wars) has shown that conventional war can also become indiscriminate in conduct and disproportionate to any valid purpose. We do not want in any way to give encouragement to a notion of "making the world safe for conventional war," which introduces its own horrors.

218. Hence, we believe that any program directed at reducing reliance on nuclear weapons is not likely to succeed unless it includes measures to reduce tensions, and to work for the balanced reduction of conventional forces. We believe that important possibilities exist which, if energetically pursued, would ensure against building up conventional forces as a concomitant of reductions in nuclear weapons. Examples are to be found in the ongoing negotiations for mutual balanced force reductions, the prospects for which are certainly not dim and would be enhanced by agreements on strategic weapons, and in the confidence-building measures still envisaged under the Helsinki agreement and review conference.

219. We must re-emphasize with all our being, nonetheless, that it is not only nuclear war that must be prevented, but war itself. Therefore, with Pope John Paul II we declare:

Today, the scale and the horror of modern warfare—whether nuclear or not—makes it totally unacceptable as a means of settling differences between nations. War should belong to the tragic past, to history; it should find no place on humanity's agenda for the future.[94]

Reason and experience tell us that a continuing upward spiral, even in conventional arms, coupled with an unbridled increase in armed forces, instead of securing true peace will almost certainly be provocative of war.

4. Civil Defense

220. Attention must be given to existing programs for civil defense against nuclear attack, including blast and fall-out shelters and relocation plans. It is unclear in the public mind whether these are intended to offer significant protection against at least some forms of nuclear attack or are being put into place to enhance the credibility of the strategic deterrent forces by demonstrating an ability to survive attack. This confusion has led to public skepticism and even ridicule of the program and casts doubt on the credibility of the government. An independent commission of scientists, engineers, and weapons experts is needed to examine if these or any other plans offer a realistic prospect of survival for the nation's population or its cherished values, which a nuclear war would presumably be fought to preserve.

5. Efforts to Develop Non-violent Means of Conflict Resolution

221. We affirm a nation's right to defend itself, its citizens, and its values. Security is the right of all, but that right, like everything else, must be subject to divine law and the limits defined by that law. We must find means of defending peoples that do not depend upon the threat of annihilation. Immoral means can never be justified by the end sought; no objective, however worthy of good in itself, can justify sinful acts or policies. Though our primary concern through this statement is war and the nuclear threat, these principles apply as well to all forms of violence, including insurgency, counter-insurgency, "destabilization," and the like.

222. a) The Second Vatican Council praised "those who renounce the use of violence in the vindication of their rights and who resort to methods of defense which are otherwise available to weaker parties, provided that this can be done without injury to the rights and duties

---

94. John Paul II, "Homily at Bagington Airport," Coventry, 2; cited, p. 55.

of others or of the community itself."[95] To make such renunciation effective and still defend what must be defended, the arts of diplomacy, negotiation, and compromise must be developed and fully exercised. Non-violent means of resistance to evil deserve much more study and consideration than they have thus far received. There have been significant instances in which people have successfully resisted oppression without recourse to arms.[96] Non-violence is not the way of the weak, the cowardly, or the impatient. Such movements have seldom gained headlines, even though they have left their mark on history. The heroic Danes who would not turn Jews over to the Nazis and the Norwegians who would not teach Nazi propaganda in schools serve as inspiring examples in the history of non-violence.

223. Non-violent resistance, like war, can take many forms depending upon the demands of a given situation. There is, for instance, organized popular defense instituted by government as part of its contingency planning. Citizens would be trained in the techniques of peaceable non-compliance and non-cooperation as a means of hindering an invading force or non-democratic government from imposing its will. Effective non-violent resistance requires the united will of a people and may demand as much patience and sacrifice from those who practice it as is now demanded by war and preparation for war. It may not always succeed. Nevertheless, before the possibility is dismissed as impractical or unrealistic, we urge that it be measured against the almost certain effects of a major war.

224. b) Non-violent resistance offers a common ground of agreement for those individuals who choose the option of Christian pacifism even to the point of accepting the need to die rather than to kill, and those who choose the option of lethal force allowed by the theology of just war. Non-violent resistance makes clear that both are able to be committed to the same objective: defense of their country.

225. c) Popular defense would go beyond conflict resolution and compromise to a basic synthesis of beliefs and values. In its practice, the objective is not only to avoid causing harm or injury to another creature, but, more positively, to seek the good of the other. Blunting the aggression of an adversary or oppressor would not be enough. The goal is winning the other over, making the adversary a friend.

---

95. *Pastoral Constitution*, #78.

96. G. Sharp, *The Politics of Nonviolent Action* (Boston: 1973); R. Fisher and W. Ury, *Getting to Yes: Negotiating Agreement Without Giving In* (Boston: 1981).

226.   It is useful to point out that these principles are thoroughly compatible with—and to some extent derived from—Christian teachings and must be part of any Christian theology of peace. Spiritual writers have helped trace the theory of non-violence to its roots in scripture and tradition and have illustrated its practice and success in their studies of the church fathers and the age of martyrs. Christ's own teachings and example provide a model way of life incorporating the truth, and a refusal to return evil for evil.

227.   Non-violent popular defense does not insure that lives would not be lost. Nevertheless, once we recognize that the almost certain consequences of existing policies and strategies of war carry with them a very real threat to the future existence of humankind itself, practical reason as well as spiritual faith demand that it be given serious consideration as an alternative course of action.

228.   d) Once again we declare that the only true defense for the world's population is the rejection of nuclear war and the conventional wars which could escalate into nuclear war. With Pope John Paul II, we call upon educational and research institutes to take a lead in conducting peace studies: "Scientific studies on war, its nature, causes, means, objectives and risks have much to teach us on the conditions for peace . . ."[97] To achieve this end, we urge that funds equivalent to a designated percentage (even one-tenth of one percent) of current budgetary allotments for military purposes be set aside to support such peace research.

229.   In 1981, the Commission on Proposals for the National Academy of Peace and Conflict Resolution recommended the establishment of the U.S. Academy of Peace, a recommendation nearly as old as this country's constitution. The commission found that "peace is a legitimate field of learning that encompasses rigorous, interdisciplinary research, education, and training directed toward peacemaking expertise."[98] We endorse the commission's recommendation and urge all citizens to support training in conflict resolution, non-violent resistance, and programs devoted to service to peace and education for peace. Such an academy would not only provide a center for peace studies and activities, but also be a tangible evidence of our nation's sincerity in its often professed commitment to international peace and the abolition of war. We urge universities, particularly Catholic

---

97. John Paul II, "World Day of Peace Message 1982," #7, cited, p. 476.

98. *To Establish the United States Academy of Peace: Report of the Commission on Proposals for the National Academy of Peace and Conflict Resolution* (Washington, D.C.: 1981), pp. 119-20.

universities, in our country to develop programs for rigorous, interdisciplinary research, education and training directed toward peacemaking expertise.

230. We, too, must be prepared to do our part to achieve these ends. We encourage churches and educational institutions, from primary schools to colleges and institutes of higher learning, to undertake similar programs at their own initiative. Every effort must be made to understand and evaluate the arms race, to encourage truly transnational perspectives on disarmament, and to explore new forms of international cooperation and exchange. No greater challenge or higher priority can be imagined than the development and perfection of a theology of peace suited to a civilization poised on the brink of self-destruction. It is our prayerful hope that this document will prove to be a starting point and inspiration for that endeavor.

6. The Role of Conscience

231. A dominant characteristic of the Second Vatican Council's evaluation of modern warfare was the stress it placed on the requirement for proper formation of conscience. Moral principles are effective restraints on power only when policies reflect them and individuals practice them. The relationship of the authority of the state and the conscience of the individual on matters of war and peace takes a new urgency in the face of the destructive nature of modern war.

232. a) In this connection we reiterate the position we took in 1980. Catholic teaching does not question the right in principle of a government to require military service of its citizens provided the government shows it is necessary. A citizen may not casually disregard his country's conscientious decision to call its citizens to acts of "legitimate defense." Moreover, the role of Christian citizens in the armed forces is a service to the common good and an exercise of the virtue of patriotism, so long as they fulfill this role within defined moral norms.[99]

233. b) At the same time, no state may demand blind obedience. Our 1980 statement urged the government to present convincing reasons for draft registration, and opposed reinstitution of conscription itself except in the case of a national defense emergency. Moreover, it reiterated our support for conscientious objection in general and for selective conscientious objection to participation in a partic-

---

99. United States Catholic Conference, *Statement on Registration and Conscription for Military Service* (Washington, D.C.: 1980). Cf. also *Human Life in Our Day*, cited, pp. 42-45.

ular war, either because of the ends being pursued or the means being used. We called selective conscientious objection a moral conclusion which can be validly derived from the classical teaching of just-war principles. We continue to insist upon respect for and legislative protection of the rights of both classes of conscientious objectors. We also approve requiring alternative service to the community—not related to military needs—by such persons.

B. Shaping a Peaceful World

234. Preventing nuclear war is a moral imperative; but the avoidance of war, nuclear or conventional, is not a sufficient conception of international relations today. Nor does it exhaust the content of Catholic teaching. Both the political needs and the moral challenge of our time require a positive conception of peace, based on a vision of a just world order. Pope Paul VI summarized classical Catholic teaching in his encyclical, *The Development of Peoples*: "Peace cannot be limited to a mere absence of war, the result of an ever precarious balance of forces. No, peace is something built up day after day, in the pursuit of an order intended by God, which implies a more perfect form of justice among men and women."[100]

1. World Order in Catholic Teaching

235. This positive conception of peace sees it as the fruit of order; order, in turn, is shaped by the values of justice, truth, freedom and love. The basis of this teaching is found in sacred scripture, St. Augustine and St. Thomas. It has found contemporary expression and development in papal teaching of this century. The popes of the nuclear age, from Pius XII through John Paul II have affirmed pursuit of international order as the way to banish the scourge of war from human affairs [101]

236. The fundamental premise of world order in Catholic teaching is a theological truth: the unity of the human family—rooted in

---

100. Paul VI, *The Development of Peoples* (1967), #76.

101. Cf. V. Yzermans, ed., *Major Addresses of Pius XII*, 2 vols. (St. Paul: 1961) and J. Gremillion, *The Gospel of Peace and Justice*, cited.

common creation, destined for the kingdom, and united by moral bonds of rights and duties. This basic truth about the unity of the human family pervades the entire teaching on war and peace: for the pacifist position it is one of the reasons why life cannot be taken, while for the just-war position, even in a justified conflict bonds of responsibility remain in spite of the conflict.

237. Catholic teaching recognizes that in modern history, at least since the Peace of Westphalia (1648) the international community has been governed by nation-states. Catholic moral theology, as expressed for example in chapters 2 and 3 of *Peace on Earth*, accords a real but relative moral value to sovereign states. The value is real because of the functions states fulfill as sources of order and authority in the political community; it is relative because boundaries of the sovereign state do not dissolve the deeper relationships of responsibility existing in the human community. Just as within nations the moral fabric of society is described in Catholic teaching in terms of reciprocal rights and duties—between individuals, and then between the individual and the state—so in the international community *Peace on Earth* defines the rights and duties which exist among states.[102]

238. In the past twenty years Catholic teaching has become increasingly specific about the content of these international rights and duties. In 1963, *Peace on Earth* sketched the political and legal order among states. In 1966, *The Development of Peoples* elaborated on order of economic rights and duties. In 1979, Pope John Paul II articulated the human rights basis of international relations in his "Address to the United Nations General Assembly."

239. These documents and others which build upon them, outlined a moral order of international relations, i.e., how the international community *should* be organized. At the same time this teaching has been sensitive to the actual pattern of relations prevailing among states. While not ignoring present geopolitical realities, one of the primary functions of Catholic teaching on world order has been to point the way toward a more integrated international system.

240. In analyzing this path toward world order, the category increasingly used in Catholic moral teaching (and, more recently, in the social sciences also) is the interdependence of the world today. The theological principle of unity has always affirmed a human interdependence; but today this bond is complemented by the growing

---

102. Cf. John XXIII, *Peace on Earth* (1963), esp. #80-145.

political and economic interdependence of the world, manifested in a whole range of international issues.[103]

241.   An important element missing from world order today is a properly constituted political authority with the capacity to shape our material interdependence in the direction of moral interdependence. Pope John XXIII stated the case in the following way:

> Today the universal common good poses problems of world-wide dimensions, which cannot be adequately tackled or solved except by the efforts of public authority endowed with a wideness of powers, structure and means of the same proportions: that is, of public authority which is in a position to operate in an effective manner on a world-wide basis. The moral order itself, therefore, demands that such a form of public authority be established.[104]

242.   Just as the nation-state was a step in the evolution of government at a time when expanding trade and new weapons technologies made the feudal system inadequate to manage conflicts and provide security, so we are now entering an era of new, global interdependencies requiring global systems of governance to manage the resulting conflicts and ensure our common security. Major global problems such as worldwide inflation, trade and payments deficits, competition over scarce resources, hunger, widespread unemployment, global environmental dangers, the growing power of transnational corporations, and the threat of international financial collapse, as well as the danger of world war resulting from these growing tensions—cannot be remedied by a single nation-state approach. They shall require the concerted effort of the whole world community. As we shall indicate below, the United Nations should be particularly considered in this effort.

243.   In the nuclear age, it is in the regulation of interstate conflicts and ultimately the replacement of military by negotiated solutions that the supreme importance and necessity of a moral as well as a political concept of the international common good can be grasped. The absence of adequate structures for addressing these issues places even greater responsiblity on the policies of individual states. By a mix of political vision and moral wisdom, states are called to interpret the national interest in light of the larger global interest.

---

103. A sampling of the policy problems and possibilities posed by interdependence can be found in: R. O. Keohane and J. S. Nye, Jr., *Power and Interdependence* (Boston: 1977); S. Hoffmann, *Primacy or World Order* (New York: 1978); The Overseas Development Council, *The U.S. and World Development* 1979; 1980; 1982 (Washington, D.C.).

104. John XXIII, *Peace on Earth* (1963), #137.

244.   We are living in a global age with problems and conflicts on a global scale. Either we shall learn to resolve these problems together, or we shall destroy one another. Mutual security and survival require a new vision of the world as one interdependent planet. We have rights and duties not only within our diverse national communities but within the larger world community.

2. The Superpowers in a Disordered World

245.   No relationship more dramatically demonstrates the fragile nature of order in international affairs today than that of the United States and the Soviet Union. These two sovereign states have avoided open war, nuclear or conventional, but they are divided by philosophy, ideology and competing ambitions. Their competition is global in scope and involves everything from comparing nuclear arsenals to printed propaganda. Both have been criticized in international meetings because of their policies in the nuclear arms race.[105]

246.   In our 1980 pastoral letter on Marxism, we sought to portray the significant differences between Christian teaching and Marxism; at the same time we addressed the need for states with different political systems to live together in an interdependent world:

> The Church recognizes the depth and dimensions of the ideological differences that divide the human race, but the urgent practical need for cooperative efforts in the human interest overrules these differences. Hence Catholic teaching seeks to avoid exacerbating the ideological opposition and to focus upon the problems requiring common efforts across the ideological divide: keeping the peace and empowering the poor.[106]

247.   We believe this passage reflects the teaching of *Peace on Earth*, the continuing call for dialogue of Pope Paul VI and the 1979 address of Pope John Paul II at the United Nations. We continue to stress this theme even while we recognize the difficulty of realizing its objectives.

248.   The difficulties are particularly severe on the issue of the arms race. For most Americans, the danger of war is commonly defined primarily in terms of the threat of Soviet military expansionism and the consequent need to deter or defend against a Soviet military threat. Many assume that the existence of this threat is

---

105. This has particularly been the case in the two U.N. Special Sessions on Disarmament, 1979, 1982.

106 United States Catholic Conference, *Marxist Communism* (Washington, D.C.: 1980), p. 19

permanent and that nothing can be done about it except to build and maintain overwhelming or at least countervailing military power.[107]
249. The fact of a Soviet threat, as well as the existence of a Soviet imperial drive for hegemony, at least in regions of major strategic interest, cannot be denied. The history of the Cold War has produced varying interpretations of which side caused which conflict, but whatever the details of history illustrate, the plain fact is that the memories of Soviet policies in Eastern Europe and recent events in Afghanistan and Poland have left their mark in the American political debate. Many peoples are forcibly kept under communist domination despite their manifest wishes to be free. Soviet power is very great. Whether the Soviet Union's pursuit of military might is motivated primarily by defensive or aggressive aims might be debated, but the effect is nevertheless to leave profoundly insecure those who must live in the shadow of that might.
250. Americans need have no illusions about the Soviet system of repression and the lack of respect in that system for human rights, or about Soviet covert operations and pro-revolutionary activities. To be sure, our own system is not without flaws. Our government has sometimes supported repressive governments in the name of preserving freedom, has carried out repugnant covert operations of its own, and remains imperfect in its domestic record of ensuring equal rights for all. At the same time, there is a difference. NATO is an

---

107. The debate on U.S.-Soviet relations is extensive; recent examples of it are found in: A. Ulam, "U.S.-Soviet Relations: Unhappy Coexistence," *America and the World, 1978; Foreign Affairs* 57 (1979):556-71; W. G. Hyland, "U.S.-Soviet Relations: The Long Road Back," *America and the World, 1981; Foreign Affairs* 60 (1982):525-50; R. Legvold, "Containment Without Confrontation," *Foreign Policy* 40 (1980):74-98; S. Hoffmann, "Muscle and Brains," *Foreign Policy* 37 (1979-80):3-27; P. Hassner, "Moscow and The Western Alliance," *Problems of Communism* 30 (1981):37-54; S. Bialer, "The Harsh Decade: Soviet Policies in the 1980s," *Foreign Affairs* 59 (1981):999-1020; G. Kennan, *The Nuclear Delusion: Soviet-American Relations in the Atomic Age* (New York: 1982); N. Podhoretz, *The Present Danger* (New York: 1980); P. Nitze, "Strategy in the 1980s," *Foreign Affairs* 59 (1980):82-101; R. Strode and C. Gray, "The Imperial Dimension of Soviet Military Power," *Problems of Communism* 30 (1981):1-15; International Institute for Strategic Studies, *Prospects of Soviet Power in the 1980s*, Parts I and II, Adelphi Papers #151 and 152 (London: 1979); S. S. Kaplan, ed., *Diplomacy of Power: Soviet Armed Forces as a Political Instrument* (Washington, D.C.: 1981); R. Barnet, *The Giants: Russia and America* (New York: 1977); M. McGwire, *Soviet Military Requirements*, The Brookings Institution (Washington, D.C.: 1982); R. Tucker, "The Purposes of American Power," *Foreign Affairs* 59 (1980/81):241-74; A. Geyer, *The Idea of Disarmament: Rethinking the Unthinkable* (Washington, D.C.: 1982). For a review of Soviet adherence to treaties cf.: "The SALT Syndrome Charges and Facts: Analysis of an 'Anti-SALT Documentary,'" report prepared by U.S. government agencies (State, Defense, CIA, ACDA and NSC), reprinted in *The Defense Monitor* 10, #8A, Center for Defense Information.

alliance of democratic countries which have freely chosen their association; the Warsaw Pact is not.

251. To pretend that as a nation we have lived up to all our own ideals would be patently dishonest. To pretend that all evils in the world have been or are now being perpetrated by dictatorial regimes would be both dishonest and absurd. But having said this, and admitting our own faults, it is imperative that we confront reality. The facts simply do not support the invidious comparisons made at times, even in our own society, between our way of life, in which most basic human rights are at least recognized even if they are not always adequately supported, and those totalitarian and tyrannical regimes in which such rights are either denied or systematically suppressed. Insofar as this is true, however, it makes the promotion of human rights in our foreign policy, as well as our domestic policy, all the more important. It is the acid test of our commitment to our democratic values. In this light, any attempts to justify, for reasons of state, support for regimes that continue to violate human rights is all the more morally reprehensible in its hypocrisy.

252. A glory of the United States is the range of political freedoms its system permits us. We, as bishops, as Catholics, as citizens, exercise those freedoms in writing this letter, with its share of criticisms of our government. We have true freedom of religion, freedom of speech, and access to a free press. We could not exercise the same freedoms in contemporary Eastern Europe or in the Soviet Union. Free people must always pay a proportionate price and run some risks—responsibly—to preserve their freedom.

253. It is one thing to recognize that the people of the world do not want war. It is quite another thing to attribute the same good .motives to regimes or political systems that have consistently demonstrated precisely the opposite in their behavior. There are political philosophies with understandings of morality so radically different from ours, that even negotiations proceed from different premises, although identical terminology may be used by both sides. This is no reason for not negotiating. It is a very good reason for not negotiating blindly or naively.

254. In this regard, Pope John Paul II offers some sober reminders concerning dialogue and peace:

> [O]ne must mention the tactical and deliberate lie, which misuses language, which has recourse to the most sophisticated techniques of propaganda, which deceives and distorts dialogue and incites to aggression . . . while certain parties are fostered by ideologies which, in spite of their declarations, are opposed to the dignity of the human person, ideologies which

see in struggle the motive force of history, that see in force the source of rights, that see in the discernment of the enemy the ABC of politics, dialogue is fixed and sterile. Or, if it still exists, it is a superficial and falsified reality. It becomes very difficult, not to say impossible, therefore. There follows almost a complete lack of communication between countries and blocs. Even the international institutions are paralyzed. And the setback to dialogue then runs the risk of serving the arms race. However, even in what can be considered as an impasse to the extent that individuals support such ideologies, the attempt to have a lucid dialogue seems still necessary in order to unblock the situation and to work for the possible establishment of peace on particular points. This is to be done by counting upon common sense, on the possibilities of danger for everyone and on the just aspirations to which the peoples themselves largely adhere.[108]

255.　The cold realism of this text, combined with the conviction that political dialogue and negotiations must be pursued, in spite of obstacles, provides solid guidance for U.S.-Soviet relations. Acknowledging all the differences between the two philosophies and political systems, the irreducible truth is that objective mutual interests do exist between the superpowers. Proof of this concrete if limited convergence of interest can be found in some vitally important agreements on nuclear weapons which have already been negotiated in the areas of nuclear testing and nuclear explosions in space as well as the SALT I agreements.

256.　The fact that the Soviet union now possesses a huge arsenal of strategic weapons as threatening to us as ours may appear to them does not exclude the possibility of success in such negotiations. The conviction of many European observers that a *modus vivendi* (often summarized as "detente") is a practical possibility in political, economic, and scientific areas should not be lightly dismissed in our country.

257.　Sensible and successful diplomacy, however, will demand that we avoid the trap of a form of anti-Sovietism which fails to grasp the central danger of a superpower rivalry in which both the U.S. and the U.S.S.R. are the players, and fails to recognize the common interest both states have in never using nuclear weapons. Some of those dangers and common interests would exist in any world where two great powers, even relatively benign ones, competed for power, influence, and security. The diplomatic requirement for addressing the U.S.-Soviet relationship is not romantic idealism about Soviet intentions and capabilities but solid realism which recognizes that everyone will lose in a nuclear exchange.

258.　As bishops we are concerned with issues which go beyond diplomatic requirements. It is of some value to keep raising in the realm

---

108. John Paul II, "World Day of Peace Message 1983," #7.

of the political debate truths which ground our involvement in the affairs of nations and peoples. Diplomatic dialogue usually sees the other as a potential or real adversary. Soviet behavior in some cases merits the adjective reprehensible, but the Soviet people and their leaders are human beings created in the image and likeness of God. To believe we are condemned in the future only to what has been the past of U.S.-Soviet relations is to underestimate both our human potential for creative diplomacy and God's action in our midst which can open the way to changes we could barely imagine. We do not intend to foster illusory ideas that the road ahead in superpower relations will be devoid of tension or that peace will be easily achieved. But we do warn against that "hardness of heart" which can close us or others to the changes needed to make the future different from the past.

3. Interdependence: From Fact to Policy

259. While the nuclear arms race focuses attention on the U.S.-Soviet relationship, it is neither politically wise nor morally justifiable to ignore the broader international context in which that relationship exists. Public attention, riveted on the big powers, often misses the plight of scores of countries and millions of people simply trying to survive. The interdependence of the world means a set of interrelated human questions. Important as keeping the peace in the nuclear age is, it does not solve or dissolve the other major problems of the day. Among these problems the pre-eminent issue is the continuing chasm in living standards between the industrialized world (East and West) and the developing world. To quote Pope John Paul II:

> So widespread is the phenomenon that it brings into question the financial, monetary, production and commercial mechanisms that, resting on various political pressures, support the world economy. These are proving incapable either of remedying the unjust social situations inherited from the past or of dealing with the urgent challenges and ethical demands of the present.[109]

260. The East-West competition, central as it is to world order and important as it is in the foreign policy debate, does not address this moral question which rivals the nuclear issue in its human significance. While the problem of the developing nations would itself require a pastoral letter, Catholic teaching has maintained an analysis of the problem which should be identified here. The analysis acknowledges internal causes of poverty, but also concentrates on the way the larger

---

109. John Paul II, "The Redeemer of Man," #16, *Origins* 8 (1980):635.

international economic structures affect the poor nations. These particularly involve trade, monetary, investment and aid policies.

261.　Neither of the superpowers is conspicuous in these areas for initiatives designed to address "the absolute poverty" in which millions live today.[110]

262.　From our perspective and experience as bishops, we believe there is a much greater potential for response to these questions in the minds and hearts of Americans than has been reflected in U.S. policy. As pastors who often appeal to our congregations for funds destined for international programs, we find good will and great generosity the prevailing characteristics. The spirit of generosity which shaped the Marshall Plan is still alive in the American public.

263.　We must discover how to translate this personal sense of generosity and compassion into support for policies which would respond to papal teaching in international economic issues. It is precisely the need to expand our conception of international charity and relief to an understanding of the need for social justice in terms of trade, aid and monetary issues which was reflected in Pope John Paul II's call to American Catholics in Yankee Stadium:

> Within the framework of your national institutions and in cooperation with all your compatriots, you will also want to seek out the structural reasons which foster or cause the different forms of poverty in the world and in your own country, so that you can apply the proper remedies. You will not allow yourselves to be intimidated or discouraged by over-simplified explanations which are more ideological than scientific—explanations which try to account for a complex evil by some single cause. But neither will you recoil before the reforms—even profound ones—of attitudes and structures that may prove necessary in order to recreate over and over again the conditions needed by the disadvantaged if they are to have a fresh chance in the hard struggle of life. The poor of the United States and of the world are your brothers and sisters in Christ.[111]

264.　The Pope's words highlight an intellectual, moral, and political challenge for the United States. Intellectually, there is a need to rethink the meaning of national interest in an interdependent world. Morally, there is a need to build upon the spirit of generosity present in the U.S. public, directing it toward a more systematic response to the major issues affecting the poor of the world. Politically, there is

---

110. The phrase and its description are found in R. S. McNamara, *Report to the Board of Governors of the World Bank* 1978; cf. also 1979; 1980 (Washington, D.C.).

111. John Paul II, "Homily at Yankee Stadium," #4, *Origins* 9 (1979):311.

a need for U.S. policies which promote the profound structural reforms called for by recent papal teaching.

265. Precisely in the name of international order papal teaching has, by word and deed, sought to promote multilateral forms of cooperation toward the developing world. The U.S. capacity for leadership in multilateral institutions is very great. We urge much more vigorous and creative response to the needs of the developing countries by the United States in these institutions.

266. The significant role the United States could play is evident in the daily agenda facing these institutions. Proposals addressing the relationship of the industrialized and developing countries on a broad spectrum of issues, all in need of "profound reforms," are regularly discussed in the United Nations and other international organizations. Without U.S. participation, significant reform and substantial change in the direction of addressing the needs of the poor will not occur. Meeting these needs is an essential element for a peaceful world.

267. Papal teaching of the last four decades has not only supported international institutions in principle, it has supported the United Nations specifically. Pope Paul VI said to the U.N. General Assembly:

> The edifice which you have constructed must never fail; it must be perfected and made equal to the needs which world history will present. You mark a stage in the development of mankind for which retreat must never be admitted, but from which it is necessary that advance be made.[112]

268. It is entirely necessary to examine the United Nations carefully, to recognize its limitations and propose changes where needed. Nevertheless, in light of the continuing endorsement found in papal teaching, we urge that the United States adopt a stronger supportive leadership role with respect to the United Nations. The growing interdependence of the nations and peoples of the world, coupled with the extra-governmental presence of multinational corporations, requires new structures of cooperation. As one of the founders of and major financial contributors to the United Nations, the United States can, and should, assume a more positive and creative role in its life today.

269. It is in the context of the United Nations that the impact of the arms race on the prospects for economic development is highlighted. The numerous U.N. studies on the relationship of development and disarmament support the judgment of Vatican II cited earlier in this letter: "The arms race is one of the greatest curses on the human

---

112. Paul VI, "Address to the General Assembly of the United Nations" (1965), #2.

race and the harm it inflicts upon the poor is more than can be endured."[113]

270.   We are aware that the precise relationship between disarmament and development is neither easily demonstrated nor easily reoriented. But the fact of a massive distortion of resources in the face of crying human need creates a moral question. In an interdependent world, the security of one nation is related to the security of all. When we consider how and what we pay for defense today, we need a broader view than the equation of arms with security.[114] The threats to the security and stability of an interdependent world are not all contained in missiles and bombers.

271.   If the arms race in all its dimensions is not reversed, resources will not be available for the human needs so evident in many parts of the globe and in our own country as well. But we also know that making resources available is a first step; policies of wise use would also have to follow. Part of the process of thinking about the economics of disarmament includes the possibilities of conversion of defense industries to other purposes. Many say the possibilities are great if the political will is present. We say the political will to reorient resources to human needs and redirect industrial, scientific, and technological capacity to meet those needs is part of the challenge of the nuclear age. Those whose livelihood is dependent upon industries which can be reoriented should rightfully expect assistance in making the transition to new forms of employment. The economic dimension of the arms race is broader than we can assess here, but these issues we have raised are among the primary questions before the nation.[115]

272.   An interdependent world requires an understanding that key policy questions today involve mutuality of interest. If the monetary and trading systems are not governed by sensitivity to mutual needs, they can be destroyed. If the protection of human rights and the promotion of human needs are left as orphans in the diplomatic arena, the stability we seek in increased armaments will eventually

---

113. *Pastoral Constitution*, #81.

114. Cf. Hoffman, cited; Independent Commission on Disarmament and Security Issues, *Common Security* (New York: 1982).

115. For an analysis of the policy problems of reallocating resources, cf: Bruce M. Russett, *The Prisoners of Insecurity* (San Francisco: 1983). Cf.: *Common Security*, cited; Russett, cited; *U.N. Report on Disarmament and Development* (New York: 1982); United Nations, *The Relationship Between Disarmament and Development: A Summary*, Fact Sheet #21 (New York: 1982).

be threatened by rights denied and needs unmet in vast sectors of the globe. If future planning about conservation of and access to resources is relegated to a pure struggle of power, we shall simply guarantee conflict in the future.

273.   The moral challenge of interdependence concerns shaping the relationships and rules of practice which will support our common need for security, welfare, and safety. The challenge tests our idea of human community, our policy analysis, and our political will. The need to prevent nuclear war is absolutely crucial, but even if this is achieved, there is much more to be done.

IV. The Pastoral Challenge and Response

A. The Church: A Community of Conscience, Prayer and Penance

274. Pope John Paul II, in his first encyclical, recalled with gratitude the teaching of Pius XII on the Church. He then went on to say:

> Membership in that body has for its source a particular call, united with the saving action of grace. Therefore, if we wish to keep in mind this community of the People of God, which is so vast and so extremely differentiated, we must see first and foremost Christ saying in a way to each member of the community: "Follow Me." It is the community of the disciples, each of whom in a different way—at times very consciously and consistently, at other times not very consciously and very consistently—is following Christ. This shows also the deeply "personal" aspect and dimension of this society.[116]

275. In the following pages we should like to spell out some of the implications of being a community of Jesus' disciples in a time when our nation is so heavily armed with nuclear weapons and is engaged in a continuing development of new weapons together with strategies for their use

276. It is clear today, perhaps more than in previous generations, that convinced Christians are a minority in nearly every country of the world—including nominally Christian and Catholic nations. In our own country we are coming to a fuller awareness that a response

---

116. John Paul II, "The Redeemer of Man," #21, cited, p. 641. Much of the following reflects the content of A. Dulles, *A Church to Believe in: Discipleship and the Dynamics of Freedom* (New York: 1982), ch. 1.

to the call of Jesus is both personal and demanding. As believers we can identify rather easily with the early Church as a company of witnesses engaged in a difficult mission. To be disciples of Jesus requires that we continually go beyond where we now are. To obey the call of Jesus means separating ourselves from all attachments and affiliation that could prevent us from hearing and following our authentic vocation. To set out on the road to discipleship is to dispose oneself for a share in the cross (cf. Jn. 16:20). To be a Christian, according to the New Testament, is not simply to believe with one's mind, but also to become a doer of the word, a wayfarer with and a witness to Jesus. This means, of course, that we never expect complete success within history and that we must regard as normal even the path of persecution and the possibility of martyrdom.

277.   We readily recognize that we live in a world that is becoming increasingly estranged from Christian values. In order to remain a Christian, one must take a resolute stand against many commonly accepted axioms of the world. To become true disciples, we must undergo a demanding course of induction into the adult Christian community. We must continually equip ourselves to profess the full faith of the Church in an increasingly secularized society. We must develop a sense of solidarity, cemented by relationships with mature and exemplary Christians who represent Christ and his way of life.

278.   All of these comments about the meaning of being a disciple or a follower of Jesus today are especially relevant to the quest for genuine peace in our time.

B. Elements of a Pastoral Response

279.   We recommend and endorse for the faithful some practical programs to meet the challenge to their faith in this area of grave concern.

1. Educational Programs and Formation of Conscience

280.   Since war, especially the threat of nuclear war, is one of the central problems of our day, how we seek to solve it could determine the mode, and even the possibility, of life on earth. God made human beings stewards of the earth; we cannot escape this responsibility. Therefore we urge every diocese and parish to implement balanced

and objective educational programs to help people at all age levels to understand better the issues of war and peace. Development and implementation of such programs must receive a high priority during the next several years. They must teach the full impact of our Christian faith. To accomplish this, this pastoral letter in its entirety, including its complexity, should be used as a guide and a framework for such programs, as they lead people to make moral decisions about the problems of war and peace, keeping in mind that the applications of principles in this pastoral letter do not carry the same moral authority as our statements of universal moral principles and formal Church teaching.

281.   In developing educational programs, we must keep in mind that questions of war and peace have a profoundly moral dimension which responsible Christians cannot ignore. They are questions of life and death. True, they also have a political dimension because they are embedded in public policy. But the fact that they are also political is no excuse for denying the Church's obligation to provide its members with the help they need in forming their consciences. We must learn together how to make correct and responsible moral judgments. We reject, therefore, criticism of the Church's concern with these issues on the ground that it "should not become involved in politics." We are called to move from discussion to witness and action.

282.   At the same time, we recognize that the Church's teaching authority does not carry the same force when it deals with technical solutions involving particular means as it does when it speaks of principles or ends. People may agree in abhorring an injustice, for instance, yet sincerely disagree as to what practical approach will achieve justice. Religious groups are as entitled as others to their opinion in such cases, but they should not claim that their opinions are the only ones that people of good will may hold.

283.   The Church's educational programs must explain clearly those principles or teachings about which there is little question. Those teachings, which seek to make explicit the gospel call to peace and the tradition of the Church, should then be applied to concrete situations. They must indicate what the possible legitimate options are and what the consequences of those options may be. While this approach should be self-evident, it needs to be emphasized. Some people who have entered the public debate on nuclear warfare, at all points on the spectrum of opinion, appear not to understand or accept some of the clear teachings of the Church as contained in papal or conciliar documents. For example, some would place almost no limits

on the use of nuclear weapons if they are needed for "self-defense.'
Some on the other side of the debate insist on conclusions which
may be legitimate options but cannot be made obligatory on the basis
of actual Church teaching.

2. True Peace Calls for "Reverence for Life"

284.   All of the values we are promoting in this letter rest ultimately
in the disarmament of the human heart and the conversion of the
human spirit to God who alone can give authentic peace. Indeed, to
have peace in our world, we must first have peace within ourselves.
As Pope John Paul II reminded us in his 1982 World Day of Peace
message, world peace will always elude us until peace becomes a
reality for each of us personally. "It springs from the dynamism of
free wills guided by reason towards the common good that is to be
attained in truth, justice and love."[117] Interior peace becomes possible
only when we have a conversion of spirit. We cannot have peace with
hate in our hearts.
285.   No society can live in peace with itself, or with the world,
without a full awareness of the worth and dignity of every human
person, and of the sacredness of all human life (Jas. 4:1-2). When
we accept violence in any form as commonplace, our sensitivities
become dulled. When we accept violence, war itself can be taken
for granted. Violence has many faces: oppression of the poor, dep-
rivation of basic human rights, economic exploitation, sexual exploitation and pornography, neglect or abuse of the aged and the
helpless, and innumerable other acts of inhumanity. Abortion in particular blunts a sense of the sacredness of human life. In a society
where the innocent unborn are killed wantonly, how can we expect
people to feel righteous revulsion at the act or threat of killing non-
combatants in war?
286.   We are well aware of the differences involved in the taking
of human life in warfare and the taking of human life through abortion.
As we have discussed throughout this document, even justifiable
defense against aggression may result in the indirect or unintended
loss of innocent human lives. This is tragic, but may conceivably be
proportionate to the values defended. Nothing, however, can justify
direct attack on innocent human life, in or out of warfare. Abortion
is precisely such an attack.

---

117. John Paul II, "World Day of Peace Message 1982," #4, cited, p. 475.

287. We know that millions of men and women of good will, of all religious persuasions, join us in our commitment to try to reduce the horrors of war, and particularly to assure that nuclear weapons will never again be used, by any nation, anywhere, for any reason. Millions join us in our "no" to nuclear war, in the certainty that nuclear war would inevitably result in the killing of millions of innocent human beings, directly or indirectly. Yet many part ways with us in our efforts to reduce the horror of abortion and our "no" to war on innocent human life in the womb, killed not indirectly, but directly.

288. We must ask how long a nation willing to extend a constitutional guarantee to the "right" to kill defenseless human beings by abortion is likely to refrain from adopting strategic warfare policies deliberately designed to kill millions of defenseless human beings, if adopting them should come to seem "expedient." Since 1973, approximately 15 million abortions have been performed in the United States, symptoms of a kind of disease of the human spirit. And we now find ourselves seriously discussing the pros and cons of such questions as infanticide, euthanasia, and the involvement of physicians in carrying out the death penalty. Those who would celebrate such a national disaster can only have blinded themselves to its reality.

289. Pope Paul VI was resolutely clear: *If you wish peace, defend life.*[118] We plead with all who would work to end the scourge of war to begin by defending life at its most defenseless, the life of the unborn.

3. Prayer

290. A conversion of our hearts and minds will make it possible for us to enter into a closer communion with our Lord. We nourish that communion by personal and communal prayer, for it is in prayer that we encounter Jesus, who is our peace, and learn from him the way to peace.

291. In prayer we are renewed in faith and confirmed in our hope in God's promise.

292. The Lord's promise is that he is in our midst when we gather in prayer. Strengthened by this conviction, we beseech the risen Christ to fill the world with his peace. We call upon Mary, the first disciple and the Queen of Peace, to intercede for us and for the people of our

---

118. Paul VI, "World Day of Peace Message 1977."

time that we may walk in the way of peace. In this context, we encouage devotion to Our Lady of Peace.

293.   As believers, we understand peace as a gift of God. This belief prompts us to pray constantly, personally and communally, particularly through the reading of scripture and devotion to the rosary, especially in the family. Through these means and others, we seek the wisdom to begin the search for peace and the courage to sustain us as instruments of Christ's peace in the world.

294.   The practice of contemplative prayer is especially valuable for advancing harmony and peace in the world. For this prayer rises, by divine grace, where there is total disarmament of the heart and unfolds in an experience of love which is the moving force of peace. Contemplation fosters a vision of the human family as united and interdependent in the mystery of God's love for all people. This silent, interior prayer bridges temporarily the "already" and "not yet," this world and God's kingdom of peace.

295.   The Mass in particular is a unique means of seeking God's help to create the conditions essential for true peace in ourselves and in the world. In the eucharist we encounter the risen Lord, who gave us his peace. He shares with us the grace of the redemption, which helps us to preserve and nourish this precious gift. Nowhere is the Church's urgent plea for peace more evident in the liturgy than in the Communion Rite. After beginning this rite of the Mass with the Lord's Prayer, praying for reconciliation now and in the kingdom to come, the community asks God to "grant us peace in our day," not just at some time in the distance future. Even before we are exhorted "to offer each other the sign of peace," the priest continues the Church's prayer for peace, recalling the Lord Jesus Christ's own legacy of peace:

> Lord Jesus Christ, you said to your apostles: I leave you peace, my peace I give you. Look not on our sins, but on the faith of your Church, and grant us the peace and unity of your kingdom.

Therefore we encourage every Catholic to make the sign of peace at Mass an authentic sign of our reconciliation with God and with one another. This sign of peace is also a visible expression of our commitment to work for peace as a Christian community. We approach the table of the Lord only after having dedicated ourselves as a Christian community to peace and reconciliation. As an added sign of commitment, we suggest that there always be a petition for peace in the general intercessions at every eucharistic celebration.

296.   We implore other Christians and everyone of good will to join us in this continuing prayer for peace, as we beseech God for

peace within ourselves, in our families and community, in our nation, and in the world.

4. Penance

297. Prayer by itself is incomplete without penance. Penance directs us toward our goal of putting on the attitudes of Jesus himself. Because we are all capable of violence, we are never totally conformed to Christ and are always in need of conversion. The twentieth century alone provides adequate evidence of our violence as individuals and as a nation. Thus, there is continual need for acts of penance and conversion. The worship of the Church, particularly through the sacrament of reconciliation and communal penance services, offers us multiple ways to make reparation for the violence in our own lives and in our world.

298. As a tangible sign of our need and desire to do penance we, for the cause of peace, commit ourselves to fast and abstinence on each Friday of the year. We call upon our people voluntarily to do penance on Friday by eating less food and by abstaining from meat. This return to a traditional practice of penance, once well observed in the U.S. Church, should be accompanied by works of charity and service toward our neighbors. Every Friday should be a day significantly devoted to prayer, penance, and almsgiving for peace.

299. It is to such forms of penance and conversion that the Scriptures summon us. In the words of the prophet Isaiah:

> Is not the sort of fast that pleases me, to break unjust fetters and undo the thongs of the yoke, to let the oppressed go free and break every yoke, to share your bread with the hungry, and shelter the homeless poor, to clothe the person you see to be naked and not turn from your own kin? Then will your light shine like the dawn and your wound be quickly healed over. If you do away with the yoke, the clenched fist, the wicked word, if you give your bread to the hungry and relief to the oppressed, your light will rise in the darkness, and your shadows become like noon (Is. 58:6-8; 10).

300. The present nuclear arms race has distracted us from the words of the prophets, has turned us from peace-making, and has focused our attention on a nuclear buildup leading to annihilation. We are called to turn back from this evil of total destruction and turn instead in prayer and penance toward God, toward our neighbor, and toward the building of a peaceful world:

> I set before you life or death, a blessing or a curse. Choose life then, so that you and your descendants may live in the love of Yahweh your God, obeying His voice, clinging to Him; for in this your life consists, and on

this depends your long stay in the land which Yahweh swore to your fathers Abraham, Isacc and Jacob, He would give them (Dt. 30:19–20).

C. Challenge and Hope

301. The arms race presents questions of conscience we may not evade. As American Catholics, we are called to express our loyalty to the deepest values we cherish: peace, justice and security for the entire human family. National goals and policies must be measured against that standard.

302. We speak here in a specific way to the Catholic community. After the passage of nearly four decades and a concomitant growth in our understanding of the ever growing horror of nuclear war, we must shape the climate of opinion which will make it possible for our country to express profound sorrow over the atomic bombing in 1945. Without that sorrow, there is no possibility of finding a way to repudiate future use of nuclear weapons or of conventional weapons in such military actions as would not fulfill just-war criteria.

303. **To Priests, Deacons, Religious and Pastoral Ministers:** We recognize the unique role in the Church which belongs to priests and deacons by reason of the sacrament of holy orders and their unique responsibility in the community of believers. We also recognize the valued and indispensable role of men and women religious. To all of them and to all other pastoral ministers we stress that the cultivation of the gospel vision of peace as a way of life for believers and as a leaven in society should be a major objective. As bishops, we are aware each day of our dependence upon your efforts. We are aware, too, that this letter and the new obligations it could present to the faithful may create difficulties for you in dealing with those you serve. We have confidence in your capacity and ability to convert these difficulties into an opportunity to give a fuller witness to our Lord and his message. This letter will be known by the faithful only as well as you know it, preach and teach it, and use it creatively.

304. **To Educators:** We have outlined in this letter Catholic teaching on war and peace, but this framework will become a living message only through your work in the Catholic community. To teach the ways of peace is not "to weaken the nation's will" but to be concerned for the nation's soul. We address theologians in a particular way, because we know that we have only begun the journey toward a theology of peace; without your specific contributions this desperately needed dimension of our faith will not be realized. Through your help we may provide new vision and wisdom for church and state.

305. We are confident that all the models of Catholic education which have served the Church and our country so well in so many ways will creatively rise to the challenge of peace.

306. **To Parents:** Your role, in our eyes, is unsurpassed by any other; the foundation of society is the family. We are conscious of the continuing sacrifices you make in the efforts to nurture the full human and spiritual growth of your children. Children hear the gospel message first from your lips. Parents who consciously discuss issues of justice in the home and who strive to help children solve conflicts through non-violent methods enable their children to grow up as peacemakers. We pledge our continuing pastoral support in the common objective we share of building a peaceful world for the future of children everywhere.

307. **To Youth:** Pope John Paul II singles you out in every country where he visits as the hope of the future; we agree with him. We call you to choose your future work and professions carefully. How you spend the rest of your lives will determine, in large part, whether there will any longer be a world as we know it. We ask you to study carefully the teachings of the Church and the demands of the gospel about war and peace. We encourage you to seek careful guidance as you reach conscientious decisions about your civic responsibilities in this age of nuclear military forces.

308. We speak to you, however, as people of faith. We share with you our deepest conviction that in the midst of the dangers and complexities of our time God is with us, working through us and sustaining us all in our efforts of building a world of peace with justice for each person.

309. **To Men and Women in Military Service:** Millions of you are Catholics serving in the armed forces. We recognize that you carry special responsibilities for the issues we have considered in this letter. Our perspective on your profession is that of Vatican II: "All those who enter the military service in loyalty to their country should look upon themselves as the custodians of the security and freedom of their fellow-countrymen; and where they carry out their duty properly, they are contributing to the maintenance of peace."[119]

---

119. *Pastoral Constitution*, #79.

310. It is surely not our intention in writing this letter to create problems for Catholics in the armed forces. Every profession, however, has its specific moral questions and it is clear that the teaching on war and peace developed in this letter poses a special challenge and opportunity to those in the military profession. Our pastoral contact with Catholics in military service, either through our direct experience or through our priests, impresses us with the demanding moral standards we already see observed and the commitment to Catholic faith we find. We are convinced that the challenges of this letter will be faced conscientiously. The purpose of defense policy is to defend the peace; military professionals should understand their vocation this way. We believe they do, and we support this view.

311. We remind all in authority and in the chain of command that their training and field manuals have long prohibited, and still do prohibit, certain actions in the conduct of war, especially those actions which inflict harm on innocent civilians. The question is not whether certain measures are unlawful or forbidden in warfare, but which measures: to refuse to take such actions is not an act of cowardice or treason but one of courage and patriotism.

312. We address particularly those involved in the exercise of authority over others. We are aware of your responsibilities and impressed by the standard of personal and professional duty you uphold. We feel, therefore, that we can urge you to do everything you can to assure that every peaceful alternative is exhausted before war is even remotely considered. In developing battle plans and weapons systems, we urge you to try to ensure that these are designed to reduce violence, destruction, suffering, and death to a minimum, keeping in mind especially non-combatants and other innocent persons.

313. Those who train individuals for military duties must remember that the citizen does not lose his or her basic human rights by entrance into military service. No one, for whatever reason, can justly treat a military person with less dignity and respect than that demanded for and deserved by every human person. One of the most difficult problems of war involves defending a free society without destroying the values that give it meaning and validity. Dehumanization of a nation's military personnel by dulling their sensibilities and generating hatred toward adversaries in an effort to increase their fighting effectiveness robs them of basic human rights and freedoms, degrading them as persons.

314. Attention must be given to the effects on military personnel themselves of the use of even legitimate means of conducting war. While attacking legitimate targets and wounding or killing opposed combat forces may be morally justified, what happens to military persons required to carry out these actions? Are they treated merely as instruments of war, insensitive as the weapons they use? With what moral or emotional experiences do they return from war and attempt to resume normal civilian lives? How does their experience affect society? How are they treated by society?

315. It is not only basic human rights of adversaries that must be respected, but those of our own forces as well. We re-emphasize, therefore, the obligation of responsible authorities to ensure appropriate training and education of combat forces and to provide appropriate support for those who have experienced combat. It is unconscionable to deprive those veterans of combat whose lives have been severely disrupted or traumatized by their combat experiences of proper psychological and other appropriate treatment and support.

316. Finally, we are grateful for the sacrifice so many in military service must make today and for the service offered in the past by veterans. We urge that those sacrifices be mitigated so far as possible by the provision of appropriate living and working conditions and adequate financial recompense. Military persons and their families must be provided continuing opportunity for full spiritual growth, the exercise of their religious faith, and a dignified mode of life.

317. We especially commend and encourage our priests in military service. In addition to the message already addressed to all priests and religious, we stress the special obligations and opportunities you face in direct pastoral service to the men and women of the armed forces. To complement a teaching document of this scope, we shall need the sensitive and wise pastoral guidance only you can provide. We promise our support in facing this challenge.

318. **To Men and Women in Defense Industries:** You also face specific questions, because the defense industry is directly involved in the development and production of the weapons of mass destruction which have concerned us in this letter. We do not presume or pretend that clear answers exist to many of the personal, professional and financial choices facing you in your varying responsibilities. In this letter we have ruled out certain uses of nuclear weapons, while also expressing conditional moral acceptance for deterrence. All Catholics, at every level of defense industries, can and should use the moral principles of this letter to form their consciences. We realize that different judgments of conscience will face different people, and we recognize the possibility of diverse concrete judgments being made in this complex area. We seek as moral teachers and pastors to be available to all who confront these questions of personal and vocational choice. Those who in conscience decide that they should no longer be associated with defense activities should find support in the Catholic community. Those who remain in these industries or earn a profit from the weapons industry should find in the Church guidance and support for the ongoing evaluation of their work.

319. **To Men and Women of Science:** At Hiroshima Pope John Paul said: "Criticism of science and technology is sometimes so severe that it comes close to condemning science itself. On the contrary, science and technology are a wonderful product of a God-given human creativity, since they have provided us with wonderful possibilities and we all gratefully benefit from them. But we know that this potential is not a neutral one: it can be used either for man's progress or for his degradation."[120] We appreciate the efforts of scientists, some of whom first unlocked the secret of atomic power and others of whom have developed it in diverse ways, to turn the enormous power of science to the cause of peace.

320. Modern history is not lacking scientists who have looked back with deep remorse on the development of weapons to which they contributed, sometimes with the highest motivation, even believing that they were creating weapons that would render all other weapons obsolete and convince the world of the unthinkableness of war. Such efforts have ever proved illusory. Surely, equivalent dedication of scientific minds to reverse current trends, and to pursue concepts as bold and adventuresome in favor of peace as those which in the past have magnified the risks of war, could result in dramatic benefits for all of humanity. We particularly note in this regard the extensive efforts of public education undertaken by physicians and scientists on the medical consequences of nuclear war.

321. We do not, however, wish to limit our remarks to the physical sciences alone. Nor do we limit our remarks to physical scientists. In his address at the United Nations University in Hiroshima, Pope John Paul II warned about misuse of "the social sciences and the human behavioral sciences when they are utilized to manipulate people, to crush their mind, souls, dignity and freedom . . ."[121] The positive role of social science in overcoming the dangers of the nuclear age is evident in this letter. We have been dependent upon the research and analysis of social scientists in our effort to apply the moral principles of the Catholic tradition to the concrete problems of our

---

12.. John Paul II, "Address to Scientists and Scholars," #3, cited, p. 621.

121. Ibid.

day. We encourage social scientists to continue this work of relating moral wisdom and political reality. We are in continuing need of your insights.

322.   **To Men and Women of the Media:** We have directly felt our dependence upon you in writing this letter; all the problems we have confronted have been analyzed daily in the media. As we have grappled with these issues, we have experienced some of the responsibility you bear for interpreting them. On the quality of your efforts depends in great measure the opportunity the general public will have for understanding this letter.

323.   **To Public Officials:** Vatican II spoke forcefully of "the difficult yet noble art of politics."[122] No public issue is more difficult than avoiding war; no public task more noble than building a secure peace. Public officials in a democracy must both lead and listen; they are ultimately dependent upon a popular consensus to sustain policy. We urge you to lead with courage and to listen to the public debate with sensitivity.

324.   Leadership in a nuclear world means examining with great care and objectivity every potential initiative toward world peace, regardless of how unpromising it might at first appear. One specific initiative which might be taken now would be the establishment of a task force including the public sector, industry, labor, economists and scientists with the mandate to consider the problems and challanges posed by nuclear disarmament to our economic well-being and industrial output. Listening includes being particularly attentive to the consciences of those who sincerely believe that they may not morally support warfare in general, a given war, or the exercise of a particular role within the armed forces. Public officials might well serve all of our fellow citizens by proposing and supporting legislation designed to give maximum protection to this precious freedom, true freedom of conscience.

325.   In response to public officials who both lead and listen, we urge citizens to respect the vocation of public service. It is a role easily maligned but not easily fulfilled. Neither justice nor peace can be achieved with stability in the absence of courageous and creative public servants.

326.   **To Catholics as Citizens:** All papal teaching on peace has stressed the crucial role of public opinion. Pope John Paul II specified the tasks before us: "There is no justification for not raising the

---

122. *Pastoral Constitution*, #75.

question of the responsibility of each nation and each individual in the face of possible wars and of the nuclear threat."[123] In a democracy, the responsibility of the nation and that of its citizens coincide. Nuclear weapons pose especially acute questions of conscience for American Catholics. As citizens we wish to affirm our loyalty to our country and its ideals, yet we are also citizens of the world who must be faithful to the universal principles proclaimed by the Church. While some other countries also possess nuclear weapons, we may not forget that the United States was the first to build and to use them. Like the Soviet Union, this country now possesses so many weapons as to imperil the continuation of civilization. Americans share responsibility for the current situation, and cannot evade responsibility for trying to resolve it.

327. The virtue of patriotism means that as citizens we respect and honor our country, but our very love and loyalty make us examine carefully and regularly its role in world affairs, asking that it live up to its full potential as an agent of peace with justice for all people.

> Citizens must cultivate a generous and loyal spirit of patriotism, but without being narrow-minded. This means that they will always direct their attention to the good of the whole human family, united by the different ties which bind together races, people, and nations.[124]

328. In a pluralistic democracy like the United States, the Church has a unique opportunity, precisely because of the strong constitutional protection of both religious freedom and freedom of speech and the press, to help call attention to the moral dimensions of public issues. In a previous pastoral letter, *Human Life In Our Day*, we said: "In our democratic system, the fundamental right of political dissent cannot be denied, nor is rational debate on public policy decisions of government in the light of moral and political principles to be discouraged. It is the duty of the governed to analyze responsibly the concrete issues of public policy."[125] In fulfilling this role, the Church helps to create a community of conscience in the wider civil community. It does this in the first instance by teaching clearly within the Church the moral principles which bind and shape the Catholic conscience. The Church also fulfills a teaching role, however, in striving to share the moral wisdom of the Catholic tradition with the larger society.

---

123. John Paul II, "Address at Hiroshima," #2, *Origins* 10 (1981):620.

124. *Pastoral Constitution*, #75.

125. *Human Life in Our Day*, cited, p. 41.

329. In the wider public discussion, we look forward in a special way to cooperating with all other Christians with whom we share common traditions. We also treasure cooperative efforts with Jewish and Islamic communities, which possess a long and abiding concern for peace as a religious and human value. Finally, we reaffirm our desire to participate in a common public effort with all men and women of good will who seek to reverse the arms race and secure the peace of the world.

CONCLUSION

330.   As we close this lengthy letter, we try to answer two key questions as directly as we can.

331.   Why do we address these matters fraught with such complexity, controversy and passion? We speak as pastors, not politicians. We are teachers, not technicians. We cannot avoid our responsibility to lift up the moral dimensions of the choices before our world and nation. The nuclear age is an era of moral as well as physical danger. We are the first generation since Genesis with the power to virtually destroy God's creation. We cannot remain silent in the face of such danger. Why do we address these issues? We are simply trying to live up to the call of Jesus to be peacemakers in our own time and situation.

332.   What are we saying? Fundamentally, we are saying that the decisions about nuclear weapons are among the most pressing moral questions of our age. While these decisions have obvious military and political aspects, they involve fundamental moral choices. In simple terms, we are saying that good ends (defending one's country, protecting freedom, etc.) cannot justify immoral means (the use of weapons which kill indiscriminately and threaten whole societies). We fear that our world and nation are headed in the wrong direction. More weapons with greater destructive potential are produced every day. More and more nations are seeking to become nuclear powers. In our quest for more and more security, we fear we are actually becoming less and less secure.

333.   In the words of our Holy Father, we need a "moral about-face." The whole world must summon the moral courage and technical means to say "no" to nuclear conflict; "no" to weapons of mass destruction; "no" to an arms race which robs the poor and the vulnerable; and "no" to the moral danger of a nuclear age which places before humankind indefensible choices of constant terror or surrender. Peacemaking is not an optional commitment. It is a requirement of our faith. We are called to be peacemakers, not by some movement of the moment, but by our Lord Jesus. The content and context of our peacemaking is set, not by some political agenda or ideological program, but by the teaching of his Church.

334. Thus far in this pastoral letter we have made suggestions we hope will be helpful in the present world crisis. Looking ahead to the long and productive future of humanity for which we all hope, we feel that a more all-inclusive and final solution is needed. We speak here of the truly effective international authority for which Pope John XXIII ardently longed in *Peace on Earth*,[126] and of which Pope Paul VI spoke to the United Nations on his visit there in 1965.[127] The hope for such a structure is not unrealistic, because the point has been reached where public opinion sees clearly that, with the massive weaponry of the present, war is no longer viable. There *is* a substitute for war. There is negotiation under the supervision of a global body realistically fashioned to do its job. It must be given the equipment to keep constant surveillance on the entire earth. Present technology makes this possible. It must have the authority, freely conferred upon it by all the nations, to investigate what seems to be preparations for war by any one of them. It must be empowered by all the nations to enforce its commands on every nation. It must be so constituted as to pose no threat to any nation's sovereignty. Obviously the creation of such a sophisticated instrumentality is a gigantic task, but is it hoping for too much to believe that the genius of humanity, aided by the grace and guidance of God, is able to accomplish it? To create it may take decades of unrelenting daily toll by the world's best minds and most devoted hearts, but it shall never come into existence unless we make a beginning now.

335. As we come to the end of our pastoral letter we boldly propose the beginning of this work. The evil of the proliferation of nuclear arms becomes more evident every day to all people. No one is exempt from their danger. If ridding the world of the weapons of war could be done easily, the whole human race would do it gladly tomorrow. Shall we shrink from the task because it is hard?

336. We turn to our own government and we beg it to propose to the United Nations that it begin this work immediately; that it

---

126. John XXIII, *Peace on Earth* (1963), #137.

127. Paul VI, "Address to the General Assembly of the United Nations," (1965), #2.

create an international task force for peace; that this task force, with membership open to every nation, meet daily through the years ahead with one sole agenda: the creation of a world that will one day be safe from war. Freed from the bondage of war that holds it captive in its threat, the world will at last be able to address its problems and to make genuine human progress, so that every day there may be more freedom, more food, and more opportunity for every human being who walks the face of the earth.

337. Let us have the courage to believe in the bright future and in a God who wills it for us—not a perfect world, but a better one. The perfect world, we Christians believe, is beyond the horizon, in an endless eternity where God will be all in all. But a better world is here for human hands and hearts and minds to make.

338. For the community of faith the risen Christ is the beginning and end of all things. For all things were created through him and all things will return to the Father through him.

339. It is our belief in the risen Christ which sustains us in confronting the awesome challenge of the nuclear arms race. Present in the beginning as the word of the Father, present in history as the word incarnate, and with us today in his word, sacraments, and spirit, he is the reason for our hope and faith. Respecting our freedom, he does not solve our problems but sustains us as we take responsibility for his work of creation and try to shape it in the ways of the kingdom. We believe his grace will never fail us. We offer this letter to the Church and to all who can draw strength and wisdom from it in the conviction that we must not fail him. We must subordinate the power of the nuclear age to human control and direct it to human benefit. As we do this we are conscious of God's continuing work among us, which will one day issue forth in the beautiful final kingdom prophesied by the seer of the Book of Revelation:

> Then I saw a new heaven and a new earth; for the first heaven and the first earth had passed away and the sea was no more. And I saw the holy city, new Jerusalem, coming down out of heaven from God, prepared as a bride adorned for her husband; and I heard a great voice from the throne saying, "Behold, the dwelling of God is with men. He will dwell with them, and they shall be his people, and God himself will be with them, he will wipe away every tear from their eyes, and death shall be no more, neither shall there be mourning nor crying nor pain any more, for the former things have passed away." And he who sat upon the throne said, "Behold, I make all things new" (Rv. 21:1-5).